THOMAS COOK
Traveller

C000318593

SYDNEY

AA

Produced by AA Publishing

Written by Anne Matthews

Series adviser: Melissa Shales

Editor: Dilys Jones

The Automobile Association would like to thank Dinah Eagle, Thomas Cook UK.

Edited, designed and produced by AA Publishing.
Maps © The Automobile Association 1993

Distributed in the United Kingdom by AA Publishing, Fanum House, Basingstoke, Hampshire, RG21 2EA.

The contents of this publication are believed correct at the time of printing. Nevertheless, the publishers cannot accept responsibility for errors or omissions, or for changes in details given. Assessments of attractions, hotels, restaurants and so forth are based upon the author's own experience and, therefore, descriptions given in this guide necessarily contain an element of subjective opinion which may not reflect the publishers' opinion or dictate a reader's own experiences on another occasion.

We have tried to ensure accuracy in this guide, but things do change and we would be grateful if readers would advise us of any inaccuracies they may encounter.

A CIP catalogue record for this book is available from the British Library.

ISBN 0 7495 0629 6

Published by The Automobile Association and the Thomas Cook Group Ltd.

This book was produced using QuarkXPress™, Aldus Freehand™ and Microsoft Word™ on Apple Macintosh™ computers.

Colour separation: BTB Colour Reproduction, Whitchurch, Hampshire

Printed by Edicoes ASA, Oporto, Portugal

Cover picture: *The Opera House, Sydney*
Title page: *Lifeguards at Avalon Beach*
Above: *Australia's koala*

Contents

Introduction   4

History   6

Discovery and Settlement   8

Geography   10

Culture and Government   12

Finding Your Feet   14

Walks and Drives   22

What to see   42

Getting Away From It All   130

Shopping   142

Entertainment   148

Sport   156

Food and Drink   162

Hotel Information   174

Practical Guide   176

Index and Acknowledgements   191

Features

Beach Life   44

Multi-cultural Sydney   50

Sydney's Architecture   58

On the Water   74

Café Life   86

Village Life   90

The Bush   102

40,000 Years of Aboriginal
  History   122

Wildlife   140

Gourmet Sydney   164

Maps

New South Wales – general   12

New South Wales within Australia   14

Sydney – city centre   16

Transport   18

New South Wales – regions   20

Walk 1 Macquarie Street to
  Circular Quay   22

Walk 2 Circular Quay West
  and The Rocks   24

Walk 3 Harbour Bridge to
  Milson's Point and Kirribilli   26

Walk 4 Paddington and Woollahra   28

Walk 5 Bondi to Bronte Beach   30

Walk 6 Watsons Bay, South Head
  and Vaucluse   32

Walk 7 Manly and North Head   34

Drive 8 The Northern Beaches   36

Drive 9 The Blue Mountains   38

Drive 10 The Southern Highlands
  and the South Coast   40

Sydney and suburbs   80

Introduction

'The best address on earth.'
'The finest harbour in the world.'
'By the standards of the world at large they live magnificently.'

*I*t's all been said, and it's true. There is a certain smugness among Sydneysiders – a self-satisfaction at having been fortunate enough to be born in, or migrated to, this young and vibrant city. Certainly, Sydney has its pollution, its industrial areas, dull suburbs and crowded highways like any other metropolis, but all this is forgiven with one glimpse of the wonderful harbour!

The pace here is less frantic than most world cities, although New South Wales country people, with their slow and tranquil lifestyle, would argue with that premise. The climate has much to do with this: hot summers defy attempts to rush about in the style of the northern hemisphere. The relatively small population also helps in creating a laid back atmosphere: Sydney is home to a mere 3.6 million people, who live in a

vast area of 1,735sq km, while the state's 5.9 million have plenty of room to breathe in an area seven times the size of England!

The city itself is spacious and surrounded by relatively unspoilt bushland, including many national parks, and 60km of beautiful, surf-pounded coastline. Sydney Harbour, the city's heart, has an amazing 240km of foreshore, a large amount of which has remained much the same as when the First Fleet made its tentative foray up

Fabulous skyline from Gladesville Bridge

the waterway in January 1788.

It is not just visitors who are excited by Sydney. There is no doubt that the locals remain enthusiastic about their city. For those who travel to work across the harbour by ferry, spend their weekends on its sandy beaches, or enjoy a picnic with a million-dollar water view, this really isn't surprising. If Sydney does not qualify as the 'best address on earth', it certainly comes close.

' . . . We got into Port Jackson early in the afternoon, and had the satisfaction of finding the finest harbour in the world . . . '
Captain Arthur Phillip, Commander of the First Fleet, on first sighting Sydney Harbour in January 1788.

'Then toast with me our happy land,
Where all that's fair prevails,
Our colour's blue and our hearts are true
In sunny New South Wales.'
Anon. Old bush song.

The world-famous Opera House

' . . . on the whole, I have to say, few cities on earth have arrived at so agreeable a fulfilment . . they are very lucky people, whose fates have washed them up upon this brave and generally decent shore.'
Jan Morris on Sydney, in *Among the Cities*, 1983.

'You feel free in Australia . . . There is a great relief in the atmosphere, a relief from tension, from pressure . . . The sky is open above you, and the air is open around you. Not the old closing-in of Europe.'
D H Lawrence, in *Kangaroo*, 1923.

' . . . From the heart of the fair city, down the vista of important streets, could be seen the wool-clippers lying at the Circular Quay. No walled prison-house of a dock that, but the integral part of the finest, most

beautiful, vast, and safe bays the sun ever shone upon.'
Joseph Conrad, in *The Mirror of The Sea*, 1906.

'Sydney is one of those places which, when a man leaves it knowing that he will never return, he cannot leave without a pang and a tear. Such is its loveliness.'
Anthony Trollope, *Australia and New Zealand*, 1873.

'At last we anchored within Sydney Cove. We found the little basin occupied by many large ships, and surrounded by warehouses. In the evening I walked through the town, and returned full of admiration at the whole scene.'
Charles Darwin, 1836 (during the voyage of HMS *Beagle*).

History

30 to 50,000 years ago
Aborigines arrive in Australia from southeast Asia and remain in total isolation from the rest of mankind until the 17th century.

1606
Dutch explorer Willem Jansz passes the west coast of Queensland – the first proof that *Terra Australis Incognita* does indeed exist.

1642
Dutch navigator Abel Tasman discovers Van Diemen's Land (Tasmania) and Staten Landt (New Zealand).

1688
William Dampier touches on the northwest coast and becomes the first Englishman to land in Australia (New Holland).

April 1770
James Cook lands at Botany Bay in the *Endeavour* and later names the eastern coast of New Holland 'New South Wales', claiming the land for King George III. The Aboriginal population of the continent is estimated at 300,000.

1779
The first suggestion that New South Wales could be used as a penal colony, following the end of British convict transportation to America in 1776.

May 1787
The First Fleet of 1,044 people in 11 ships, including 759 convicts, sets sail from Portsmouth.

January 1788
The Fleet arrives in Botany Bay, and subsequently Sydney Cove, and European settlement commences under the command of Captain Arthur Phillip.

November 1788
West of Sydney, Parramatta is founded as the centre of the colony's agricultural district.

June 1790
The struggling colony is faced with starvation, but is saved by the arrival of a supply ship from England. The Second Fleet arrives with 1,006 convicts.

1791
Arrival of the first Irish convicts in the Third Fleet.

1793
The first free settlers arrive. Elizabeth Farm, Australia's oldest surviving building, is constructed at Parramatta.

1794
The Windsor region is founded.

1795
Coal is discovered at Newcastle.

1797
George Bass explores the NSW coast and lands at Kiama.

1804
A settlement is established at Hobart, Tasmania. Uprising of 400 Irish convicts at Castle Hill, near Parramatta.

1806
Captain William Bligh, former *Bounty* commander, is made Governor of New South Wales.

1808
The Rum Rebellion and overthrow of Bligh.

1810
Lachlan Macquarie becomes Governor (1810–1821) and the colony of New South Wales begins to take shape.

1813
Explorers Blaxland, Lawson and Wentworth finally discover a route to the

farming lands of the west, over the previously impenetrable Blue Mountains.

1819

NSW population reaches 26,000 and includes almost 10,000 convicts. Hyde Park Barracks completed.

1824

Brisbane, the capital of Queensland, is founded.

1828

First census: 36,000 convicts and free settlers; 2,549 military personnel.

1829

Perth and Fremantle founded: later in the year, Western Australia is proclaimed a British colony.

1831

Assisted emigration programme initiated. In the next 20 years over 200,000 people emigrate.

1835

Elizabeth Bay House built. Foundation of Melbourne.

1836

The beginnings of settlement in Adelaide and South Australia.

1840

Convict transportation to New South Wales ceases.

1843

The first New South Wales legislature with elected members meets in Sydney.

1850

Sydney University founded.

1851

Discovery of gold near Bathurst, west of the Blue Mountains, sparks off a NSW gold rush.

1859

Queensland is proclaimed a separate colony and splits from New South Wales.

1883

Silver discovered at Broken Hill, in the far west of NSW.

1888

Sydney celebrates its centenary. Opening of Centennial Park.

1891

Establishment of the Australian Labour Party.

1900

Bubonic plague breaks out in the crowded and unsanitary Rocks region.

January 1901

Proclamation of the Commonwealth of Australia. Edmund Barton elected as the first Prime Minister.

1908

Canberra chosen as the site of the new national capital.

1923

Construction of the Sydney Harbour Bridge begins.

1927

Seat of national government moves to Canberra from Melbourne.

1932

Sydney Harbour Bridge opened.

1947

Post-war European migration programme begins in earnest.

1954

First visit to Sydney by Queen Elizabeth II.

1973

Sydney Opera House opened.

1975

Dismissal of the Whitlam government.

1981

300m high Sydney Tower, the highest public building in the southern hemisphere, completed.

1988

Australia celebrates 200 years of European settlement.

1992

Sydney's 150th anniversary of its establishment as a city.

Discovery and Settlement

*M*an had long believed in the existence of some vast southern land, but it was not until 1606 that Dutch explorer Willem Jansz passed the Queensland coast and confirmed that there was, indeed, land in these uncharted southern seas. Throughout the 17th century, many others sailed by the land that had become known as New Holland, but saw little to arouse more than a passing interest.

It was a middle-aged Englishman who changed the destiny of this southern land for ever. In 1770 a Yorkshire explorer and navigator, Captain James Cook, sailed east from Tahiti with his crew in the *Endeavour* and landed at Botany Bay, to the south of Sydney. The continent had been properly 'discovered' at last. The Englishmen were delighted with their find: the land looked promising, and there was an astounding array of unknown plants, animals and birds for scientific investigation. Cook later sailed on up the east coast and the land was claimed for King George III, under the name of New South Wales.

Firing the salute on Botany Bay's Bare Island is a reminder of colonial days

James Cook made a careful observation of the natives. He noted that these naked, wild-looking people took little interest in the visitors and wrote prophetically in his diary: 'All they seemed to want was for us to be gone'. For the Aborigines, the arrival of the well-intentioned Cook and his party must have been an enormous shock. For around 45,000 years the natives of Australia had lived their hunting, fishing and gathering lives in total isolation, unaware of the outside world.

Until the revolution of 1776, the American colonies had been used for penal purposes, and in the late 1770s, suggestions were made that New South Wales could fulfil the same role. By 1787 the plan had been finalised.

In May 1787 the First Fleet of 1,044 people, including 759 convicts, 191 of whom were women, set sail from Portsmouth under the command of Captain Arthur Phillip. Eight months later the 11 ships arrived in Botany Bay, having travelled 22,530km via Tenerife, Rio de Janeiro and Cape Town. They were not pleased with the scene that greeted them on 20 January 1788 – a barren and windswept bay which held little of the promise that Cook had intimated. Necessity drove the Fleet further north in search of a more suitable site, and six days later the ships arrived in Port Jackson, described by Captain Phillip as: 'The finest harbour in the world'.

Although the environment here at Sydney Cove was better, the early days of the colony were harsh. Poor food rations, difficulty in growing crops and the fact that anticipated supply ships did not arrive led to near starvation. The atmosphere was explosive. No one wanted to be here: the marines were homesick and the convicts probably

THOMAS COOK'S SYDNEY
Thomas Cook took his first World Tour in 1872–3, taking in Australia, and from that time on organised trips to Australia became popular. By 1888 Cook's had an office in Sydney, organising excursions for tourists arriving from Britain and the US, as well as expatriates and other travellers coming from Egypt and India. Travellers from Britain in those days took a ferry to the Continent and then went by train either to Marseille or Brindisi, where they caught a steamer to Australia, sailing via the new Suez Canal.

wished they had been hanged instead.

Despite this shaky start, the colony slowly took root. Phillip was replaced by Governor Macquarie, the 'Father of Australia', in 1810. In the next 11 years New South Wales was transformed: streets were laid out and fine buildings erected. Convict transportation continued to NSW until 1840, but free settlers began to arrive in 1819, and from 1831 to 1850 over 200,000 government-assisted migrants flocked into the colony to begin a new life in the southern sunshine – far removed from the urban nightmare of 19th-century Britain.

The discovery of gold in NSW in the 1850s brought a new wave of settlers, an influx which continued throughout the remainder of the century. In 1901 the country became the Commonwealth of Australia, and by 1925 the population of the Sydney region had exceeded 1 million. Sydney, New South Wales, and the rest of Australia have never looked back.

Geography

*D*espite its vast 801,600 sq km size (seven times larger than England), New South Wales makes up a mere 10 per cent of the Australian land mass and is only the country's fourth largest state. Cross-state distances are still considerable: from Sydney it is 1,157km west to Broken Hill, almost on the South Australian border; Tweed Heads, which borders Queensland in the north, is 908km away; and it is a 498km journey south to Eden, the last main town before Victoria.

Snowfall in Perisher Valley, NSW

The geography of New South Wales is best explained as a series of parallel strips. The fertile coastal plain, which runs the length of the state, varies in width from 30km to 80km.

This region is crossed by many small rivers and contains the major cities of Sydney, Newcastle and Wollongong, as well as the bulk of the state's population. Rising behind this plain is the Great Dividing Range, the natural barrier which caused such frustration to the early settlers in their attempts to push west for new agricultural land.

This watershed is a series of hills and ranges, which vary both in height and concentration. Major towns and cities such as Armidale, Glen Innes and Inverell are located in the northern section, while in the south of the state the range reaches its peak in Mount Kosciusko, the continent's highest point

at 2,228m.

Beyond the range, the hinterland stretches west in the form of broad plains and gently undulating slopes. This is the state's richest agricultural land, yielding cotton, wool, beef, mutton, rice, fruit and vegetables, and vast amounts of wheat. Most of the state's larger towns and population centres such as Bathurst, Orange, Dubbo and Wagga Wagga are found here.

Further west, past some indefinable line, fertile farming land ends and the outback begins. Stretching north and west to the Queensland and South Australian borders respectively, this vast, dry, sun-baked region is sparsely populated and, with the exception of the major mining centre of Broken Hill, supports only tiny settlements. Despite the region's dryness, the slow moving Darling River flows through the far west – and this is sheep-farming land. The outback, however, contains its own riches in the form of mineral deposits and the much sought after opal.

Australia's largest river network, the Murray/Murrumbidgee, flows through the more fertile land of southern NSW. The Murray also forms the greater part of the NSW/Victoria border.

The soils of New South Wales yield a bountiful crop. Agricultural products

A land of prosperous rural farms

include timber, wheat, wool, mutton, dairy products, cotton, rice, fruit, poultry and sugar. Mineral riches in the form of gold, silver, copper, zinc, lead, asbestos, mineral sands and coal are also plentiful. The ocean and rivers, too, provide a wide variety of produce, including prawns and many succulent and exotic fish unfamiliar to people of the northern hemisphere.

CLIMATE

The climate varies considerably between different parts of the state. The north is semi-tropical and experiences a Queensland-type climate: high humidity with hot summers and warm winters, while in winter there are heavy snowfalls in the southern mountains, near the Victoria border. Climatic extremes are the norm out west, in the deserts of the Broken Hill/Tibooburra region. Temperatures here can reach the mid-40s (°C) in summer, yet winter nights are chilly. Many parts of the state west of the Great Dividing Range experience irregular flooding and drought.

Sydney itself has a warm temperate climate: warm to hot summers – the mercury can soar to as high as 42°C – and mild winters. Rain patterns are often unpredictable, but most precipitation falls in the winter months from June to early September: semi-tropical summer thunderstorms are also common. The average annual Sydney rainfall is 1,216mm. Humidity reaches high levels from December to late February.

Harvest from sea as well as land

Culture and Government

Although the earliest British settlers brought with them the manners and customs of the old country, this culture inevitably became eroded by the new ideas of a unique and developing society.

Slowly but surely, speech patterns altered, intermarriage between the different classes became common, and the social 'rules' changed. In addition, by the 1850s the population was already a cultural hotch-potch, setting the scene for Australia's modern day multi-culturalism. The original Anglo-Saxon and Celtic settlers were joined by American whalers, Chinese prospectors, and French, Russian and Jewish migrants seeking a new life.

GOVERNMENT

The Australian government is modelled on the British parliamentary system, but it has two quite distinct levels of government: federal and state. Although the federal government makes decisions which affect the entire nation, the second level of rule and legislation creates a diversity from state to state in domestic affairs. New South Wales may therefore follow a different law enforcement policy to that of Queensland, or the state's education system can be different to Tasmania's. Sydney is the capital of New South Wales and the seat of the State Government. As with the federal government, each state has its own premier, cabinet and ministry. Additionally, Australia has a Governor General.

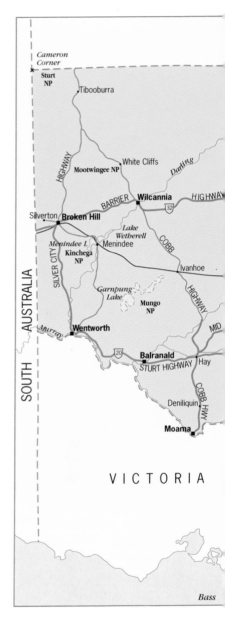

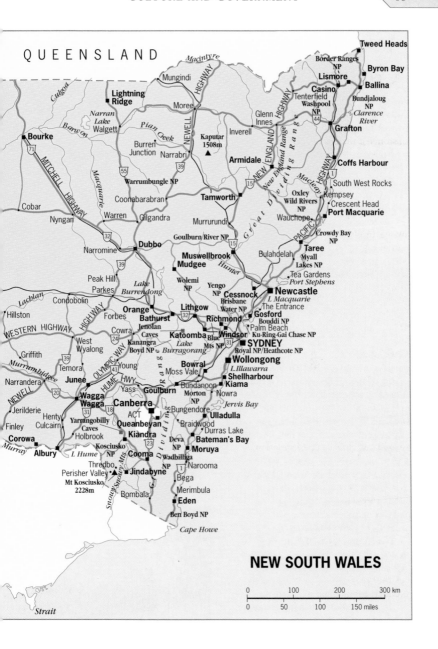

QUEENSLAND

Tweed Heads
Border Ranges NP
Byron Bay
Lismore
Ballina
Casino
Tenterfield
Washpool NP
Bundjaloug NP
Clarence River
Grafton

Macintyre
HIGHWAY

Mungindi

Lightning Ridge
Moree

Narran Lake
Walgett

Pian Creek

Glenn Innes

NEWELL HIGHWAY

NEW ENGLAND HIGHWAY

Coffs Harbour

Bourke

Culgoa

Barwon

Burren Junction
Narrabri

Kaputar 1508m ▲

Inverell

Armidale

New England Range

Great Dividing Range

South West Rocks
Kempsey
Crescent Head
Port Macquarie

MITCHELL HIGHWAY

Macquarie

Warrumbungle NP

Tamworth

Oxley Wild Rivers NP

Wauchope

Macleay

PACIFIC

Cobar

Coonabarabran

Nyngan
Warren
Gilgandra

Murrurundi

Crowdy Bay NP

Taree
Myall Lakes NP

Narromine

Dubbo

Goulburn River NP

Muswellbrook
Mudgee

Bulahdelah

Hunter

Tea Gardens
Port Stephens

Lachlan

Peak Hill
Parkes

Lake Burrendong

Wolemi NP

Yengo NP

Cessnock
Brisbane Water NP

Newcastle
L. Macquarie
The Entrance

Condobolin
Hillston

Orange

Lithgow

Gosford
Bouddi NP
Palm Beach
Ku-Ring-Gai Chase NP

WESTERN HIGHWAY

Forbes

Bathurst
Jenolan Caves

Richmond
Windsor

Cowra

Kanangra Boyd NP

Katoomba
Blue Mts NP

SYDNEY
Royal NP/Heathcote NP

Griffith
West Wyalong

Young

Lake Burragorang

Bowral
Moss Vale

Wollongong
L.Illawarra

Murrumbidgee

Temora

Junee

OLYMPIC WAY

HUME HWY

Yass

Goulburn

Bundanoon
Morton NP
Nowra

Shellharbour
Kiama

Narrandera

NEWELL

Wagga Wagga

Canberra
ACT

Bungendore

Jervis Bay

Jerilderie

Henty
Culcairn

Yarrangobilly Caves

Queanbeyan
Kiandra

Braidwood

Ulladulla

Finley

Holbrook

Deva NP

Bateman's Bay

Durras Lake

Corowa

Albury

Murray

L. Hume

Kosciusko NP

Cooma

Moruya

Great Dividing Range

Thredbo
Perisher Valley
Mt Kosciusko 2228m

Snowy Snowy Mts

Jindabyne

Wadbilliga NP

Narooma

Bega

Bombala

Merimbula

Eden

Ben Boyd NP

Cape Howe

Strait

NEW SOUTH WALES

0	100	200	300 km
0	50	100	150 miles

Finding your feet

*I*n its 200-year history, European Australia has developed its own very distinctive atmosphere, customs, language and habits – Sydney and New South Wales are no exception. Visitors from the northern hemisphere may initially be surprised by the relaxed attitude and character of the state and its residents, but it is an atmosphere which takes little getting used to, especially if you are on holiday.

Attitudes

Perhaps it is due to the state's pioneer past that there is little need to stand on ceremony here. It also seems that the rather stiff attitudes and manners of old England have been transformed by two centuries of southern sun and fresh sea breezes into a new informality. Australians are a friendly, easy-going bunch, but they don't hesitate to call a spade a spade, or greet the visitor without a formal introduction. Men are likely to be addressed as 'mate' – the universal Aussie salutation!

There's also no need to overdress here. Except for the most formal occasions – perhaps a night at the Opera House – casual clothes are the order of the day. Summer visitors will soon understand why.

Temperatures are generally around the 25–30° C mark, but can soar to over 40°C, combined with high humidity, and no one wants to pile on the clothes. Don't be surprised to see business men wearing long shorts and short-sleeved shirts.

The incredible influx of immigrants since World War II has led to a truly multi-cultural society, particularly evident in Sydney. The city streets contain a colourful blend of Aboriginal, Asian, Anglo-Saxon, Celtic, southern European, Middle Eastern and Pacific Islander – faces, colourings and clothing of all descriptions which add greatly to Sydney's cosmopolitan atmosphere. This variety is also expressed in the city's wonderful range of food and drink: everything from spicy Thai food to *gelato* or Wiener schnitzels.

GETTING AROUND

Visitors find that Sydney is an easy place to get around. The Central Business

A view of the Blue Mountains

Spectacular Sydney Tower, Centrepoint

District (CBD) is small and most of the major attractions such as the Harbour and Bridge, Opera House and the historic Rocks are all within walking distance of the shopping centre. The beaches and harbour surburbs are well-served by buses and ferries – there is nothing more delightful than sightseeing from the water. Further afield, the vast metropolitan region has good train services and you can always hire a car to visit Pittwater, the Royal National Park or the Blue Mountains. Getting around the rest of the state is easy too. Bus and train services are comfortable, not too expensive, and frequent.

The best way to orientate yourself on arrival in Sydney is to head for Sydney Tower – the city's tallest construction at over 300m high. From this lofty perch you can see the entire city spread out below, and even as far as the Blue Mountains, some 100km away. Once you've done that, get down there and enjoy the wonderful things that Sydney has to offer.

Bus

The city's bus services are particularly useful for inner city travel, and for reaching areas such as the harbour suburbs of Rose Bay, Vaucluse and Watsons Bay that are not serviced by trains.

Ferry

This is by far the most pleasant way to get around. Ferry services operate from Circular Quay to the north side of the harbour, and also to some inner west and inner east destinations. Ferries are also a cheap and fun way to do some general harbour sightseeing.

Ferries are a good way to see the sights

Rail

Sydney has an excellent rail network, which covers most of the metropolitan area. Trains run throughout the inner-city region and east to Bondi Junction. To the north, there are services to Hornsby and on to Gosford and the Central Coast, while southbound trains operate to the Royal National Park and continue on to Wollongong. To the west, trains cover the major centres of Strathfield, Parramatta and Penrith and then on to the Blue Mountains. Sydney does not have an underground system as such, although the City Circle line is below ground level.

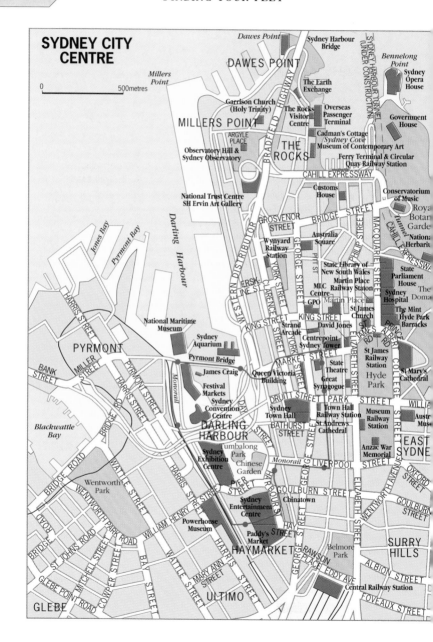

SYDNEY CITY CENTRE

0   500metres

Dawes Point

Sydney Harbour Bridge

SYDNEY HARBOUR TUNNEL (UNDER CONSTRUCTION)

Bennelong Point

Sydney Opera House

DAWES POINT

Millers Point

The Earth Exchange

Garrison Church (Holy Trinity)

The Rocks Visitor Centre

Overseas Passenger Terminal

Government House

MILLERS POINT

ARGYLE PLACE

Cadman's Cottage
Sydney Cove
Museum of Contemporary Art

THE ROCKS

Observatory Hill & Sydney Observatory

BRADFIELD HIGHWAY

Ferry Terminal & Circular Quay Railway Station

CAHILL EXPRESSWAY

Customs House

Conservatorium of Music

National Trust Centre
SH Ervin Art Gallery

Darling Harbour

Jones Bay

Pyrmont Bay

Royal Botanic Gardens

National Herbarium

GROSVENOR STREET

BRIDGE STREET

Australia Square

Wynyard Railway Station

State Library of New South Wales

Martin Place

State Parliament House

WESTERN DISTRIBUTOR

ERSKINE ST

GEORGE STREET

PITT ST

MLC Centre

Martin Place Railway Station

Sydney Hospital

The Domain

GPO

Martin Place

CLARENCE ST

National Maritime Museum

St James Church

The Mint

Hyde Park Barracks

PYRMONT

Sydney Aquarium

YORK STREET

KING STREET

Strand Arcade

David Jones

Pyrmont Bridge

HARRIS STREET

MILLER STREET

BANK STREET

Centrepoint Sydney Tower

James Craig

Queen Victoria Building

MARKET STREET

State Theatre

St James Railway Station

St Mary's Cathedral

Blackwattle Bay

Festival Markets

Sydney Convention Centre

Great Synagogue

Hyde Park

PYRMONT STREET

PYRMONT BRIDGE ROAD

Monorail

DARLING HARBOUR

DRUITT STREET

PARK STREET

ELIZABETH STREET

Sydney Town Hall

Town Hall Railway Station

Museum Railway Station

EAST SYDNEY

Wentworth Park

BATHURST STREET

St Andrews Cathedral

Australian Museum

BRIDGE ROAD

Sydney Exhibition Centre

Tumbalong Park

Chinese Garden

Monorail

LIVERPOOL STREET

Anzac War Memorial

WILLIAM STREET

HARRIS STREET

WATTLE STREET

PIER STREET

Sydney Entertainment Centre

GOULBURN STREET

Chinatown

OXFORD STREET

GOULBURN STREET

BRIDGE ROAD

WENTWORTH PARK ROAD

WILLIAM HENRY

Powerhouse Museum

HAY STREET

SURRY HILLS

ST JOHNS ROAD

MITCHELL STREET

COWPER STREET

BAY STREET

WATTLE STREET

MARY ANN STREET

Paddy's Market

HAYMARKET

GEORGE STREET

RAWSON PLACE

Belmore Park

ALBION STREET

GLEBE POINT ROAD

GLEBE

ULTIMO

EDDY AVE

Central Railway Station

FOVEAUX STREET

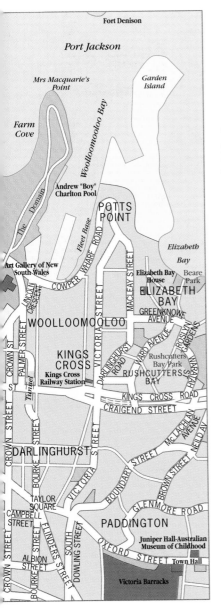

Fort Denison

Port Jackson

Mrs Macquarie's Point

Garden Island

Farm Cove

Woolloomooloo Bay

The Domain

Andrew "Boy" Charlton Pool

Fleet Base

POTTS POINT

Elizabeth Bay

Art Gallery of New South Wales

COWPER WHARF ROAD

LINCOLN CRESCENT

MACLEAY STREET

Elizabeth Bay House Beare Park

ELIZABETH BAY

VICTORIA STREET

GREENKNOWE AVENUE

WOOLLOOMOOLOO

CROWN ST

PALMER STREET

KINGS CROSS

Kings Cross Railway Station

DARLINGHURST ROAD

WARD AVENUE

ROSLYN GARDENS

Rushcutters Bay Park

INARRA ST

RUSHCUTTERS BAY

Tunnel

KINGS CROSS ROAD

CRAIGEND STREET

CROWN STREET

BOURKE STREET

VICTORIA STREET

MCLACHLAN AVENUE

NEILD AV

DARLINGHURST

STREET

BROWN STREET

TAYLOR SQUARE

CAMPBELL STREET

FLINDERS STREET

VICTORIA STREET

BOUNDARY STREET

GLENMORE ROAD

PADDINGTON

SOUTH DOWLING STREET

Juniper Hall-Australian Museum of Childhood

ALBION STREET

OXFORD STREET

Town Hall

CROWN STREET

BOURKE STREET

Victoria Barracks

Sydney's Inner Suburbs

CITY CENTRE

Sydney's mostly modern CBD (Central Business District) contains the usual range of shops, high-rise office blocks and pedestrian malls, but the central area also includes The Rocks, the Opera House, the Harbour Bridge, the Botanic Gardens, Darling Harbour and the major museums and galleries – all areas which are a must on the tourist list.

EASTERN SUBURBS

From the slightly seedy inner suburbs of Woolloomooloo, Kings Cross and Darlinghurst, to expensive harbourside areas such as Darling Point and Vaucluse, or beachside enclaves like Bondi, the eastern suburbs contain perhaps the city's most attractive and desirable districts.

INNER WEST AND SOUTH

The inner west includes Sydney University, the historic suburbs of Glebe, Balmain and Birchgrove, docklands and many colourful working-class and ethnic regions.

LOWER NORTH SHORE

This region, to the north of the Harbour Bridge, includes such contrasting areas as the North Sydney concrete and steel business district and beachside Balmoral. Other harbourside suburbs such as Kirribilli, Milson's Point and McMahons Point are both historic and picturesque.

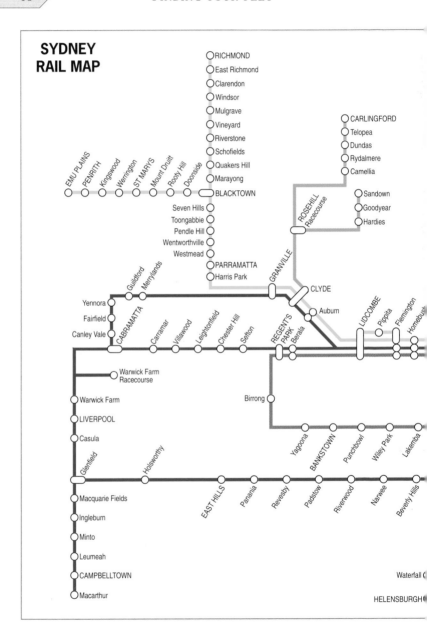

SYDNEY RAIL MAP

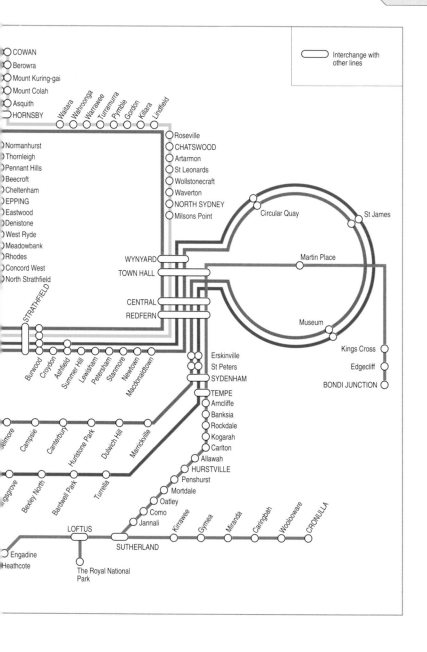

Interchange with other lines

COWAN
Berowra
Mount Kuring-gai
Mount Colah
Asquith
HORNSBY

Waitara
Wahroonga
Warrawee
Turramurra
Pymble
Gordon
Killara
Lindfield

Normanhurst
Thornleigh
Pennant Hills
Beecroft
Cheltenham
EPPING
Eastwood
Denistone
West Ryde
Meadowbank
Rhodes
Concord West
North Strathfield

Roseville
CHATSWOOD
Artarmon
St Leonards
Wollstonecraft
Waverton
NORTH SYDNEY
Milsons Point

Circular Quay
St James

WYNYARD
TOWN HALL

Martin Place

CENTRAL
REDFERN

Museum

STRATHFIELD

Kings Cross
Edgecliff
BONDI JUNCTION

Burwood
Croydon
Ashfield
Summer Hill
Lewisham
Petersham
Stanmore
Newtown
Macdonaldtown

Erskinville
St Peters
SYDENHAM
TEMPE
Arncliffe
Banksia
Rockdale
Kogarah
Carlton
Allawah
HURSTVILLE
Penshurst
Mortdale
Oatley
Como
Jannali

Belmore
Campsie
Canterbury
Hurlstone Park
Dulwich Hill
Marrickville

Kingsgrove
Bexley North
Bardwell Park
Turrella

Kirrawee
Gymea
Miranda
Caringbah
Woolooware
CRONULLA

LOFTUS
SUTHERLAND

Engadine
Heathcote

The Royal National Park

Sydney's Outer Suburbs

NORTH

This region is mostly residential, but there are large shopping and business centres at Chatswood and Hornsby, and much of the north is bushland. Ku-ring-gai Chase National Park is located here. On the ocean side lie beautiful beaches and Pittwater.

PARRAMATTA REGION

Parramatta is the geographical centre of the metropolitan area. West is mostly unattractive suburbs, but Parramatta is pleasant and contains many historic buildings.

SOUTH

This part of Sydney spreads to the Royal National Park, some 36km to the south and encompasses historic Botany Bay, the airport, many industrial regions and the attractive Georges River area.

THE FAR WEST

Beyond Parramatta, the remainder of the vast Sydney region stretches to the Blue Mountains, some 70km away. In the north, the Richmond/Windsor area is of great historic interest, while the south contains the large centres of Liverpool and Campbelltown.

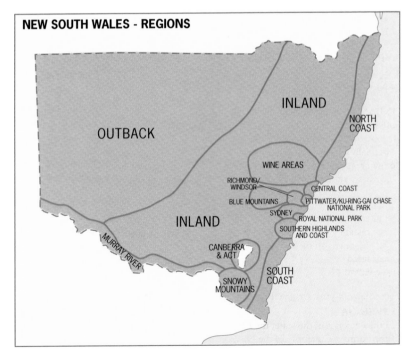

NEW SOUTH WALES - REGIONS

INLAND

NORTH COAST

OUTBACK

WINE AREAS

RICHMOND/ WINDSOR

CENTRAL COAST

BLUE MOUNTAINS

PITTWATER/KU-RING-GAI CHASE NATIONAL PARK

SYDNEY

INLAND

ROYAL NATIONAL PARK

SOUTHERN HIGHLANDS AND COAST

MURRAY RIVER

CANBERRA & ACT

SOUTH COAST

SNOWY MOUNTAINS

Regions of New South Wales

BLUE MOUNTAINS

Beginning 100km to the west of Sydney, this is one of the city's favourite recreation areas. The mountains consist of a sandstone plateau crossed by deep, heavily forested valleys.

CANBERRA AND THE ACT

Although geographically part of NSW, Canberra and the surrounding Australian Capital Territory (ACT) are administered separately. The national capital is around 300km southwest of Sydney.

CENTRAL COAST

This region starts immediately to the north of Sydney. The area is quite heavily populated and includes Newcastle, the state's second largest city, 170km north of the state capital.

INLAND

Inland NSW is a vast region, west of the Great Dividing Range, which essentially excludes the outback and other areas that are defined here. This is the state's agricultural heartland.

ISLANDS

Semi-tropical Lord Howe Island and more distant Norfolk Island lie out in the Pacific Ocean. Although Lord Howe is considered part of NSW, Norfolk Island is an external Australian territory.

MURRAY RIVER AND THE RIVERINA

In the far south of the state, the Murray River forms the majority of the NSW/Victoria boundary. The area north of the river is a fertile agricultural region known as the Riverina, containing settlements such as Albury, some 570km from Sydney.

NORTH COAST

Stretching from Newcastle to Queensland, the north coast contains some of the state's most popular beach resorts.

OUTBACK

There are always differences of opinion as to where the outback starts, but essentially it includes the northwest portion of NSW, stretching as far as Tibooburra, some 1,500km from Sydney.

SNOWY MOUNTAINS

The Great Dividing Range, which runs the length of the state, reaches its peak in the Snowy Mountains, in southeast NSW.

SOUTH COAST

The south coast's small towns and lovely beaches stretch from Wollongong, to the Victorian border at Cape Howe, well over 500km south of Sydney.

SOUTHERN HIGHLANDS

Fertile agricultural land is dotted with historic towns, which were some of the state's earliest inland settlements.

WINE AREAS

These are mainly centred on the Hunter Valley and Mudgee, to the northwest of Newcastle. Other regions are around Albury and Griffith in the state's south.

Macquarie Street to Circular Quay

This walk covers Sydney's most elegant street and takes you through harbourside parks and gardens to the Opera House (see pages 52-3, 60-1 and 76-9). *Allow 2 hours*

Nearby

Mint Museum

Hyde Park Barracks

Art Gallery of NSW

St Mary's Cathedral

Begin from the eastern side of Circular Quay and walk up Alfred Street, turn right and immediately left up Albert Street to the northern end of Macquarie Street, then turn right.

1 MACQUARIE STREET

This elegant avenue began life as a rough track, but by the end of the 19th century it had become the pride of Sydney. To the left lie the Botanic Gardens and, at the junction of Bridge Street, the gothic-style State Conservatorium of Music designed by Francis Greenway (1819). Further on, there is the imposing 1910 State Library and Mitchell Library where the street joins the Cahill Expressway, and then Parliament House (1810–16) with its attractive colonial style façade. Other buildings on the left include the Sydney Hospital (completed in 1894), the Mint Museum (1816), and finally the 1819 Hyde Park Barracks. The right-hand side of Macquarie Street has some interesting 19th-century houses and, opposite the Barracks, Francis Greenway's graceful St James Church, dating from 1822.
Turn left past the Barracks and follow the road around into Art Gallery Road.

2 THE DOMAIN

The large park which now greets the eye is known as the Domain. First designated as a park in 1810 by Governor Macquarie, it remains one of the inner city's most pleasant recreation areas. To the right, the grand Victorian building is the Art Gallery of New South Wales. Continue

across the bridge which spans the Cahill
Expressway and take the right-hand fork
in the road – this leads into the northern
extension of the Domain. On the right is
Woolloomooloo Bay, with its historic
'Finger Wharf' and naval Fleet Base.
Further on, you will pass the Andrew 'Boy'
Charlton swimming pool (see page 52).
Continue on this road until you reach the
end of the point.

3 MRS MACQUARIE'S POINT

This spot is named after the wife of an
early NSW governor – a seat is carved
out of the rock here, where she liked to
sit during the early 1800s. From the
point there are marvellous views of the
harbour, Farm Cove and the Opera
House (see page 52).
Continue around the point and on to the
Farm Cove side of Mrs Macquarie's Road.
Descend the steps on the right.

4 ROYAL BOTANIC GARDENS

You are now in the 30-hectare area of
greenery which hugs Farm Cove and
makes up the Royal Botanic Gardens.
The colony's first farm was established
here and the area was turned into
gardens between 1816 and 1831.
Attractions include tropical greenhouses,
a lake, rose garden, visitor centre and

restaurant. On a rise near the Opera
House is the Gothic Government House,
official residence of the Governor of
New South Wales (see page 53).
After exploring the Gardens, take the path
that follows Farm Cove and walk towards
the Opera House through the large iron gates.

5 SYDNEY OPERA HOUSE

Sydney's modern wonder of the world is
now in front of you. Opened in 1973,
the Opera House is a miracle of design
and construction. A walk around the
outside is needed to appreciate the
architecture, and guided tours are
available for those who would like to
explore the interior (see pages 76-7).
Follow the walkway around Sydney Cove,
back to Circular Quay.

6 CIRCULAR QUAY

This area is the hub of the city's ferry
transport system and has several outdoor
cafés at which to sit and rest. Among the
modern buildings in the area behind the
Quay is the 1885 sandstone Customs
House. This is near the spot where the
British flag was raised by the new arrivals
in 1788.
You have now returned to the start of the walk.

Take a break at Circular Quay

Circular Quay West and The Rocks

This walk takes in the highlights of Sydney's most historic area, and is a must for all visitors (see pages 64-9 and 78-9). *Allow 2 hours minimum*

Nearby

The Story of Sydney

The Earth Exchange

Dawes Point Park

Sydney Harbour

   Bridge walkway

National Trust

   Centre

S H Ervin Gallery

Begin from Circular Quay, just in front of the ferry wharves, and walk along the left-hand side of Sydney Cove.

1 CIRCULAR QUAY WEST

This area contains the Museum of Contemporary Art (see page 55) and the Overseas Passenger Terminal – take the escalator to the top level for good views of the Harbour. Across the road from the terminal is a small whitewashed house. This is Cadman's Cottage (1816) – the city's oldest building.
From here, take the steps up to George Street and turn right.

2 UPPER GEORGE STREET

Opposite the steps are Unwins Stores, dating from 1844; a little further on is the Federation-style Observer Hotel. On the right,

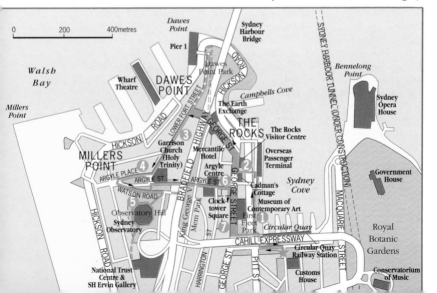

at no 104, is The Rocks Visitor Centre. Across the street are several interesting 19th-century terraced houses, such as the 1844 Counting House (no 43), and the 1915 Mercantile Hotel. Also in George Street are the Earth Exchange (a geological and mining musem – see page 63) and the Story of Sydney display.
From upper George Street there is a possible short detour to Dawes Point Park. Turn right under the Bridge and walk across the park to Hickson Road and good Harbour and Bridge views. Otherwise, continue to the end of George Street and turn left.

3 LOWER FORT STREET

Lower Fort Street contains some of the city's most attractive Georgian and Victorian terraced houses. The small Colonial House Museum is located at no 53, and a little further on you pass the atmospheric sandstone Hero of Waterloo Hotel (1844) – Sydney's second oldest pub.
At the end of this street, turn right into Argyle Place.

4 ARGYLE PLACE, MILLER'S POINT

This is Sydney's only true village green and is flanked by 19th-century terraced houses. To the left is the 1840 Garrison Church, and on the right-hand side, at the end of the green, is the Lord Nelson Hotel (1834), Sydney's oldest pub.
From here, walk around the green and turn into Watson Road, continuing up to Observatory Hill.

5 OBSERVATORY HILL

The city's highest point contains the 1858 Sydney Observatory and the remnants of Fort Phillip – the wall to the east of the observatory dates from 1804. Behind the observatory, a path leads to

the National Trust Centre and the S H Ervin Gallery.
Return to Watson Road and take the steps down to Argyle Street.

Sydney's oldest surviving house

6 ARGYLE AND HARRINGTON STREETS

Pass under the Harbour Bridge approaches and rejoin George Street at the bottom of the hill. On the left is the Argyle Centre (dating from 1828), originally an old sandstone warehouse complex, while to the right Clocktower Square is a modern shopping precinct. Next to the Argyle Centre is historic Playfair Street and The Rocks Square, with its 'First Impressions' statue.
A short detour down Harrington Street takes you into Suez Canal and Nurses' Walk – small lanes to the left which convey an idea of how The Rocks looked in the 1870s. Otherwise, continue down the hill to George Street and turn right.

7 LOWER GEORGE STREET

To the left is the Museum of Contemporary Art, while the right-hand side of the road contains a range of shops and restaurants, many located in historic buildings.
Turn left, under the railway line, into First Fleet Park to return to Circular Quay.

Harbour Bridge to Milson's Point and Kirribilli

Within close proximity is North Sydney (see pages 72–3).

This is a walk which takes in wonderful Harbour views, an interesting suburb with historic houses, and a short ferry ride home. This walk can be undertaken in combination with a visit to The Rocks. *Allow 2 hours*

Start from the Harbour Bridge pedestrian walkway entrance – reached via the Argyle Stairs (off Argyle Street) in The Rocks, then Cumberland Street.

1 SYDNEY HARBOUR BRIDGE

The pedestrian walkway follows the right-hand side of the Bridge, alongside the eight traffic lanes. From the walkway the views down into the Harbour are magnificent.

Work began on the bridge's construction in 1923 and it was opened in 1932. It is the world's widest long-span bridge: the main span is 502.9m in length and it measures 48.8m in width. The top of the arch is some 134m above the water (see pages 72-3). Sydneysiders call it the 'Coathanger'.

2 THE PYLON LOOKOUT

For an even more spectacular view (if that's possible!), call in at the Pylon Lookout on the southern side of the bridge. This is open from 10am to 5pm daily, mid-October to mid-February – at other times of the year from Saturday to Tuesday inclusive. The 200-step elevation above the walkway gives a real bird's-eye view of the harbour.

Leave the Harbour Bridge by the stairs leading to Broughton Street in Milson's

Point. Turn left under the bridge, then left again into Alfred Street.

3 MILSON'S POINT

Nowadays this small suburb is an appendage of North Sydney's business district. Walk down the hill to the end of Alfred Street and the North Sydney Olympic Swimming Pool. There is a good view of the inner harbour and western side of the Bridge from the walkway in front of the pool.

The now defunct Luna Park funpark is to the right.

Walk across the park under the Bridge and enter Kirribilli Avenue, marked by St Aloysius College on the left. Continue along this street until you turn into Waruda Avenue on the right.

4 KIRRIBILLI

This attractive harbourside suburb is a quiet enclave next to the bustle of North Sydney. From Waruda Avenue, turn right into Waruda Street and walk a short distance to Mary Booth Lookout. This park gives an excellent, close-up view of the eastern side of the Harbour Bridge, and the Opera House across the water.

Walk back along Waruda Street to reach the steps on the left at the end. At the top, turn right into Kirribilli Avenue.

5 ADMIRALTY HOUSE AND KIRRIBILLI HOUSE

You are now outside the Admiralty House gates. This is the grand Sydney residence (1846) of Australia's Governor General. A little further on, the more modest Kirribilli House is used by the Prime Minister when he is in Sydney. Both houses are open to the public only on special occasions.

Walk to the end of Kirribilli Avenue to a small park named Lady Gowrie

Attractive Kirribilli Street

Lookout. From here there are good views of Cremorne Point and the harbour.

Return to Circular Quay by ferry from Kirribilli Wharf – from Kirribilli Avenue turn right into Carabella Street, then right again into Holbrook Avenue. Otherwise, continue along Carabella Street, turn right into Peel Street and then left into Elamang Avenue.

6 CAREENING COVE

At the end of Peel Street there is a reserve with views of the cove – this is next to the Royal Sydney Yacht Squadron, one of the city's most exclusive sailing clubs. Further along Elamang Avenue you pass the Ensemble Theatre, finally reaching Milson Park which borders Careening Cove and the marina.

Either walk back to Kirribilli Wharf, or continue to Milson's Point station to return to the city by train – walk up McDougall Street, then turn left into Broughton Street, which leads to the station.

Paddington and Woollahra

This stroll takes you through two of Sydney's most colourful suburbs, and also provides plenty of shopping opportunities (see pages 88-9). *Allow 2 hours (includes some shopping time)*

Nearby

Victoria Barracks

Australian Centre for Photography

Centennial Park – optional

Start from Taylor Square, reached by buses 378 and 380 from Circular Quay and the city.

1 TAYLOR SQUARE

This is one of the inner city's major intersections, with roads leading to Paddington, Kings Cross, the city and the airport. On the left-hand side is the Classical-style 19th-century Darlinghurst Court House.

From the square, keep walking up the gradual rise to upper Oxford Street.

2 OXFORD STREET, PADDINGTON

On the right is the Academy Twin Cinema, which screens 'alternative' films. A little further on is a long sandstone wall; this is the beginning of the Victoria Barracks complex. Begun in 1841, the verandahed, sandstone barracks are still used by the army and are a fine example of Regency architecture. The next important building on the right, marked by its clock tower, is Paddington Town Hall, completed in 1891. On the left is the

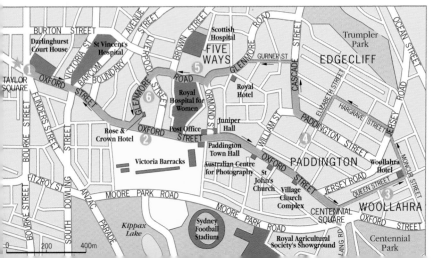

1885 Paddington Post Office. Across Ormond Street from here you will see a large, two-storey colonial-style house. This is Juniper Hall, dating from 1824 and now housing a National Trust shop and the Museum of Australian Childhood.

The next section of Oxford Street contains many interesting clothing, book and souvenir shops. On the right hand side, at no 257, is the Australian Centre for Photography, which also has a gallery and bookshop. Further along, the sandstone church on the right is St John's Presbyterian Church, dating from the 1840s. The New Edition Bookshop (opposite the church, at no 328) has free copies of a useful little book on Paddington. The next church on the right is the Village Church complex and the site of the colourful Saturday Paddington Bazaar.
At the far end of Oxford Street, turn left into Queen Street. An option is to cross Oxford Street and enter Centennial Park via the gate near Lang Road.

3 QUEEN STREET, WOOLLAHRA

This is one of the area's most leafy and exclusive streets, containing many antiques, book and rare print shops. At the next main junction, turn left into Moncur Street – marked by the red brick post office on the right, and to the left, the popular Woollahra Hotel, which has a nice beer garden.
Walk down Moncur Street, then turn right into Jersey Road. Turn left into Hargrave Street.

4 PADDINGTON'S STREETS

This is the heart of residential Paddington. The suburb is characterised by row upon row of attractively painted terraced houses which are famous for their beautiful wrought-iron lacework.

Walk along Hargrave Street, then turn left into Elizabeth Street, right into Paddington Street and right again into Cascade Street. This residential road, with its brightly coloured houses that tumble down the hill, has some particularly fine examples of lacework. *Halfway along Cascade Street, turn left into Gurner Street and continue on to Five Ways.*

Aussie troops at Victoria Barracks

5 FIVE WAYS

The shopping centre of Paddington village is full of interesting delicatessens, boutiques and restaurants. The verandahed Royal Hotel of 1888 is a wonderful example of Australian pub architecture, as well as being a good spot for a drink break.
Leave Five Ways via Glenmore Road and continue along this meandering street.

6 GLENMORE ROAD

Glenmore Road contains more terraced houses, and a few classically Sydney-style sandstone residences – for example nos 61 and 45, on the left. Just before reaching Oxford Street, also on the left, the Rose and Crown Hotel is an English-style pub dating from 1850.
Glenmore Road ends at Oxford Street – opposite the Victoria Barracks. From here you can board a bus back to the city centre.

Bondi to Bronte Beach

This is an easy 3km ocean and cliffside walk which can be combined with a day in the sun at either beach (see page 42). *Allow 1 hour*

Nearby

Bronte Park

Marks Park

Take the train from Town Hall to Bondi Junction station, then bus no 380 to the southern end of Bondi Beach – alight at the top of the hill, before you reach the beach.

1 CAMPBELL PARADE, BONDI

From the top of the hill there is an excellent view of Bondi: the beach and Ben Buckler Head at the north end, as well as the shops and buildings of Campbell Parade, which follows the curve of the beach.

Walk to the end of Campbell Parade, then turn right on to the paved walkway which backs the beach.

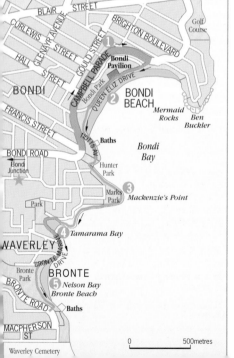

2 BONDI BEACH

This is Australia's most famous patch of sand. The name Bondi is derived from 'boondi', an Aboriginal word which, appropriately, means the sound of tumbling waters. This 1km long surf-pounded beach is the haunt of sunbathers, swimmers and surfboard riders, and part of the enduring Australian surf lifesaving tradition.

On summer weekends visitors are likely to encounter one of the many colourful surf carnivals. On the right is the Bondi Pavilion which contains food and drink outlets and often holds festivals, art exhibitions and other events.

There is, however, a large drug scene in and around Bondi Beach and travellers should avoid being out late in this area; theft is frequent.

At the southern end of the beach take the path which leads up a grassy slope, past the toilet block, and turn left into Notts Avenue.

Bondi Beach is synonymous with the healthy outdoor image of modern Australia

3 MACKENZIE'S POINT

Walk past the swimming baths – this is the home of the famous Bondi Icebergs, who swim every day of the year, no matter how cold it is! Turn left, down some steps, into the small Hunter Park and continue, past homes with million-dollar views, on the coastal path to MacKenzie's Point. The lookout here provides wonderful views of Bondi and the ocean and there is a pleasant park.
Continue on the cliff path, following it around the shore until you reach the next beach.

4 TAMARAMA BAY

This small sheltered bay, which is off limits for surfboard riders, is a popular sunbathing spot, but the currents can be treacherous. There is a surf lifesaving post here and, behind the beach, a small park, toilets and a kiosk which sells refreshments.
Walk diagonally across the park and turn left, up the steps on to Bronte Marine Drive. Follow this road to the next bay.

5 BRONTE BEACH

This is another attractive beach – commonly referred to as Bronte, but officially called Nelson Bay – which is particularly popular with families. The swimming is generally safe here and there is also an ocean pool for children. The area behind the beach has a park, with a playground and barbecue facilities, and there are shops and cafés near by.
From Macpherson Street, at the southern end of the beach, you can catch bus no 378 back to Bondi Junction station.

Bondi has a thriving beach culture

Watsons Bay, South Head and Vaucluse

Explore the historic village of Watsons Bay, South Head and the harbourside suburb of Vaucluse, combined with a ferry trip (see page 139). *Allow 45 minutes for Watsons Bay and South Head: 2 hours if you continue to Parsley Bay, Vaucluse House and Nielsen Park*

At weekends, catch the Watsons Bay Ferry from Circular Quay – this travels via Taronga Zoo and Rose Bay. At other times, take bus nos 324 or 325 from the Quay, or Kings Cross, to the Watsons Bay terminus. Make your way to the Watsons Bay Hotel, just behind the wharf.

Nearby

Vaucluse House

Nielsen Park and

beach

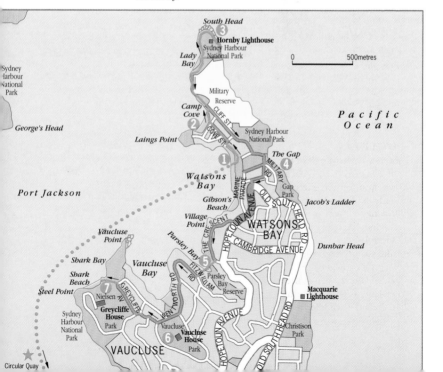

1 WATSONS BAY

In the early days of the colony, Watsons Bay was established as a fishing village and military base – a road was built to the village from Sydney Cove in 1811, and the suburb still contains some cottages dating back to the 1840s.
From the hotel, turn right into Marine Parade (along the waterfront) and right again into Short Street. A left turn down Cove Street brings you to Camp Cove.

Sydney Harbour National Park, South Head

2 CAMP COVE

This attractive cove is named after the military base, located on the hill above. It is a pretty beach with safe swimming.
To the right of the beach a stairway leads to South Head. Turn left at the top.

3 SOUTH HEAD

You are now entering part of the Sydney Harbour National Park. Walk along the cliff track until you come to Lady Bay. Commonly known as Lady Jane, this is one of Sydney's most popular nude beaches. Continue along the path to reach South Head. This rocky outcrop guards the southern approach to Port Jackson and is capped by the Hornby Lighthouse. Directly across the Harbour lies Manly and dramatic North Head, while to the left is Middle Head.
Walk around the head and return to Camp Cove, then go straight on into Cliff Street and turn left into Military Road. Walk to the top of the grassy slope in front of you.

4 THE GAP

The cliff here plunges dramatically into the Pacific Ocean and has a grim reputation as one of Sydney's most frequented suicide spots.
Walk back down to the village. Either return to Circular Quay by ferry or bus, or continue on to Vaucluse. If this is the case, make your way into Hopetoun Avenue. From here, turn right into The Crescent and continue until you reach the next bay.

5 PARSLEY BAY

Parsley Bay is another pretty harbour beach with safe swimming. It is crossed by a bridge leading from The Crescent to Fitzwilliam Road. You are now in Vaucluse, which contains some of Sydney's most palatial homes.
From Fitzwilliam Road, round the point and turn into Wentworth Road. This leads to Vaucluse Bay, and, on the left, the entrance to Vaucluse House and Park.

6 VAUCLUSE HOUSE

This gothic-style mansion dates from the 1830s and is set in a lovely garden. It is open to the public Tuesday to Sunday and contains a pleasant tea-room.
From outside Vaucluse House you can take bus no 325 back to the city. Alternatively, continue along Wentworth Road and turn right into Greycliffe Avenue. This leads to Nielsen Park and the beach.

7 NIELSEN PARK

This section of Sydney Harbour National Park contains a popular beach and tea-rooms.
Take bus no 325 from Greycliffe Avenue back to the city.

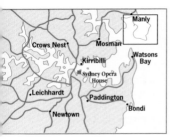

Manly and North Head

A scenic cross-harbour ferry ride takes you to Manly's beaches, followed by a walk to North Head with its spectacular harbour views (see page 139). *Allow 2 hours*

Nearby

Manly Wharf and

Fun Park

Manly Oceanarium

Take the fast Jetcat, or the ferry, from Circular Quay to Manly Wharf.

1 MANLY

Although Manly (so named by Governor Phillip in 1788 because of the 'manly' appearance of the natives) was the scene of many hostile meetings between the British and Aborigines in the early days of the colony, it was not until the 1820s that a fishing settlement grew up. A ferry service commenced in 1854, and from the late 19th century Manly became a seaside resort for Sydney city dwellers. Today, the peninsular suburb maintains this role, even though it is so close to the city. Its attract-

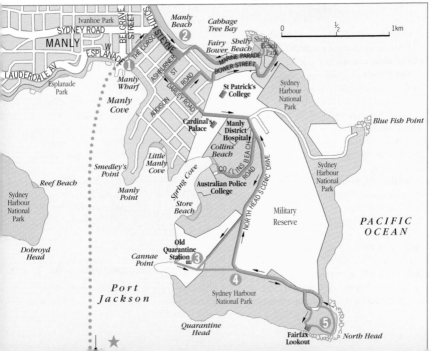

ive beaches, shops, hotels and restaurants make it a favourite stop. *From the wharf, cross the road and walk along The Corso to Manly Beach.*

2 MANLY'S BEACHES

At the end of The Corso (markets are held here on Saturdays and Sundays) is the main beach, which borders the Pacific Ocean. It is divided into three areas – Queenscliff, North Steyne and South Steyne and is one of Sydney's best and most popular surfing spots. South Steyne is flanked by shops and cafés and you can call in at the Manly Visitor's Bureau here for more information on the area. At the southern end there are two delightfully named, sheltered coves – Fairy Bower and Shelly Beach – which can be visited as a short side trip on the return from North Head. The latter has an excellent beachside restaurant. There are also several beaches on the harbour side of the peninsula (see page 43). *From the south end of the main beach, turn right into Ashburner Street, then left into Darley Road and follow this until you pass Manly District Hospital. Turn right into Collins Beach Road.*

3 OLD QUARANTINE STATION

This road leads to the Police College, from where a track goes down to Collins Beach – an optional side trip. It was on this beach that Governor Phillip was speared by Aborigines in 1790. By continuing past the Collins Beach turnoff, you will come to the now defunct Quarantine Station, which is open to the public on weekdays. The station was set up in the 1830s to isolate immigrants who were suspected of carrying infectious diseases such as smallpox or cholera, and closed in 1984. The complex contains accommodation quarters, a hospital,

mortuary, cemetery and a wharf. *From here the road continues on to the National Park and North Head.*

4 SYDNEY HARBOUR NATIONAL PARK

This heathland area is a section of the Sydney Harbour National Park, which was gazetted in 1975. It was long occupied by the Aboriginal Kamergal clan, who have left behind many ancient rock carvings. Much of the clifftop is occupied by an off-limits military reserve which will eventually become part of the park. *The Scenic Drive takes you to North Head's lookout.*

5 NORTH HEAD

This vast, rocky cliff marks the northern edge of Port Jackson and guards the entrance to the harbour. At the end of the point, Fairfax Lookout provides marvellous views of South Head, the Pacific Ocean and Sydney Harbour. There is also a footpath in front of the lookout, which takes you closer to the cliff edge. *Return to Manly via the Scenic Drive and Darley Road. An option is to turn right from here into Addison Road and right again into Bower Street, which leads to Shelly Beach. From here you can walk along Marine Parade back to the main beach.*

All the fun of the fair at Manly Cove

The Northern Beaches

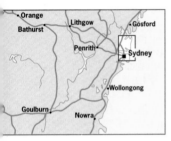

This scenic drive takes you along Sydney's northern coast and the Barrenjoey Peninsula, to the picturesque suburb of Palm Beach (see page 43). *Allow a full day*

Nearby

Balmoral Beach

Manly and its beaches

Curl Curl Beach

Start by crossing the Harbour Bridge to the north shore, then take the Manly exit off the freeway. You will pass through the suburbs of Neutral Bay, Cremorne and Mosman, before arriving at the Spit Bridge. From here, follow the signs to Brookvale, at which point you join Pittwater Road.

1 DEE WHY AND LONG REEF

The first of many surf beaches that you will encounter, Dee Why is backed by a native flora reserve and lagoon, which divides this beach from neighbouring Long Reef. Behind this stretch of sand lies a headland with a popular, scenic golf course.

2 COLLAROY AND NARRABEEN

The next two beaches merge, to form a long, peninsular finger of oceanfront that is dotted with surf clubs. At the northern end, just south of the head, the Narrabeen Lakes emerge into the ocean. Both beaches are popular with families and have ocean pools.

From Narrabeen, continue along Pittwater Road until you reach Mona Vale, where there is yet another beach: take a right turn into Barrenjoey Road here. This road takes you all the way to Palm Beach.

3 NEWPORT AND BILGOLA

Newport has an excellent beach with a surf club and pool, and, on the Pittwater side, yacht clubs, marinas and wharves. This is also the home of the Newport

Arms Hotel – a great place to take a drink or lunch break. The shopping centre, like that of Avalon, is worth a look around. The next beach to the north is the smaller, sheltered Bilgola.

Clifftop houses, Avalon Beach

4 AVALON

This is another good surf beach, with a rock pool for children, although it gets particularly crowded in summer. The shopping centre is interesting, with many art, craft and jewellery shops to serve the rather 'alternative' community which has developed here. From the centre, there is the option of driving into Avalon Parade to Clareville to view Pittwater. *Just north of Avalon, turn right off Barrenjoey Road into Whale Beach Road.*

5 WHALE BEACH

This scenic back route takes you to lovely Whale Beach and then follows the cliff, past some of the area's most attractive homes, finally descending to Palm Beach.

6 PALM BEACH

Palm Beach has much to offer: a surf beach, other beaches on the inland (Pittwater) side of the peninsula, a walk to Barrenjoey Head and its 1881 lighthouse, shops, restaurants and ferry trips across Pittwater to the shores of Ku-ring-gai Chase National Park. The

area has some very attractive and exclusive homes, many of which are owned by artists, media people and writers. The shopping centre is good for browsing, and for lunch, the famous Palm Beach fish and chips are highly recommended. *Return via Barrenjoey Road to Mona Vale, then turn right along Pittwater Road to Church Point.*

7 CHURCH POINT AND PITTWATER

From the small village of Church Point there is a good view of Pittwater and, directly in front of the jetty, Scotland Island. To the left lie the wooded slopes of Ku-ring-gai Chase National Park. From Church Point, ferries travel to Lovett Bay, Scotland Island and various other Pittwater locations. *Return to Mona Vale via Pittwater Road, and before Narrabeen turn right into the Wakehurst Parkway.*

8 NARRABEEN LAKES

The road hugs the side of this large lake – a popular venue for sailboarding and other watersports. The Parkway then passes through semi-bushland, remarkable considering its proximity to the city, to rejoin the Sydney road at Seaforth.

Riding the surf at Avalon Beach

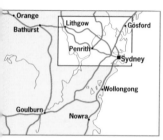

The Blue Mountains

The Blue Mountains drive allows you to explore some of the region's most dramatic scenery, combined with visits to picturesque towns and villages (see pages 96-7). *Allow a full day for a brief look or, to fully explore the area, stay overnight in the mountains*

Nearby

Parramatta

Richmond

Windsor

From the city, drive west along Parramatta Road to Concord and then take the F32 Freeway to Penrith and Emu Plains, following road signs to Katoomba. Once past Emu Plains you have reached the lower Blue Mountains.

1 LOWER BLUE MOUNTAINS

As the road winds its way up the mountains, following the path of the railway line, it passes through some small but interesting towns. Blaxland, Lawson and Wentworth Falls are named after the three explorers who discovered a route over the mountains in 1813. On the highway at Glenbrook there is a Visitor Centre and some excellent views out into the Blue Mountains National Park; the Wentworth Falls are also worth seeing.

Continue along the Great Western Highway to the Leura turnoff.

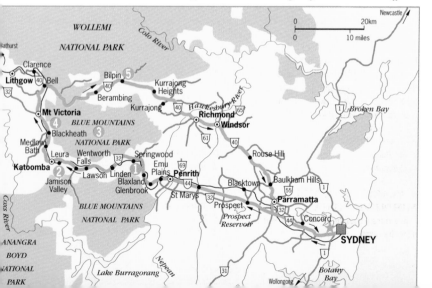

2 LEURA AND KATOOMBA

Leura is undoubtedly the region's prettiest town. The main street is full of historic buildings, many of which now contain art, craft and antiques shops, as well as some good tea-rooms and cafés. From here, you can follow the Blue Mountains Scenic Drive to Katoomba, the main town of the region.

Once in Katoomba, head for Echo Point to view the Three Sisters – a spectacular rock formation in the Jamison Valley. There are numerous lookouts into this dramatic valley, which is part of the Blue Mountains National Park. Katoomba's steep main street is full of tea-rooms and interesting shops – be sure to pay a visit to the art deco-style Paragon Café.

For full information on the area call in at the Tourist Authority office at Echo Point.

3 BLUE MOUNTAINS NATIONAL PARK

This rugged 250,000-hectare national park is composed mainly of sandstone, eroded over millions of years by rivers and creeks, which have formed dramatic valleys and sheer escarpments. These valleys are thickly forested with eucalypts, while the plateau-top heathland is home to hundreds of species of wildflowers. Aboriginal people lived in the area at least 14,000 years ago and have left their mark in the form of rock carvings and drawings. For visitors with time to spare, a short bushwalk in the park is highly recommended.

From Katoomba, continue to follow the highway northwest.

4 BLACKHEATH AND MOUNT VICTORIA

After passing through Medlow Bath, with its ornate Hydro Majestic Hotel

The dramatic Three Sisters

(1880–1903), you reach Blackheath. From here there are excellent lookout points into the Grose Valley, the national park's northern section – head for Govetts Leap and Evans Lookout. Mount Victoria, the next town, is National Trust classified and has an interesting hotel, a fine tea-shop and many antiques shops.

From Mount Victoria there is an option, if you are staying for a weekend, to visit Jenolan Caves (see page 96).

From Mount Victoria turn right on to the Bell road.

5 BELL'S LINE OF ROAD AND BILPIN

This offers an alternative, more scenic, route back to the city. From the village of Bell, the road snakes its way down the mountains, between the Blue Mountains and Wollemi national parks. *En route* are Mount Tomah Botanic Garden (near Bilpin) and various private gardens which are often open to the public. The road passes through small settlements such as Bilpin (famous for its apples) and Kurrajong Heights, and returns to Sydney via the historic towns of Richmond and Windsor (see pages 104-5).

Follow route 40 (the Windsor road) and rejoin the freeway to Sydney at Parramatta.

The Southern Highlands and the South Coast

This excursion includes the gentle rural scenery and picturesque towns of the Southern Highlands, and a visit to the beautiful south coast. *Allow a full day*

Nearby

Bundanoon

Morton National Park

Royal National Park

Leave Sydney via Parramatta Road and turn left at Ashfield, on to the Hume Highway. Continue past Liverpool, Campbelltown and Camden to Mittagong.

1 MITTAGONG

This is the gateway to the Southern Highlands region – 110km south of Sydney. Mittagong dates from the 1840s and contains several interesting old houses.

Continue along the Hume Highway, then take the Berrima turnoff.

2 BERRIMA

Historic Berrima was founded in 1829 and is the region's most picturesque village. It contains many beautifully restored sandstone buildings dating from the 1830s onwards, including the Court House and Gaol (1838–9), Holy Trinity Church (1847–9) and the 1834 Surveyor General Hotel. In addition, there are many craft and home produce shops and an abundance of tea-rooms and cafés.

Leave Berrima by the Moss Vale road.

3 MOSS VALE

This attractive town is a popular tourist centre and a target for people retiring from the frantic pace of city life. It has a couple of historic houses, lovely gardens, and many interesting antiques shops.

Near by, the hamlet of Sutton Forest is full of grand 1880s country houses. From Moss Vale there is also an option to drive on to the village of Bundanoon and Morton National Park.
Take the Highlands Highway north to Bowral.

4 BOWRAL

This resort town was founded in 1862 and has some impressive houses and attractive gardens. A highlight is the Sir Donald Bradman Museum, located in the town's cricket pavilion – the cricketing legend was born here in 1908.
From here, follow the road to Glenquarry and then on to Avoca and Fitzroy Falls.

The awesome beauty of Fitzroy Falls

5 FITZROY FALLS

These spectacular falls, located just off the road, plunge 180m into the Shoalhaven River and rugged valley below. From the lookout, there are fine views into Kangaroo Valley.
From the Falls, follow the scenic Kangaroo Valley road to the top of the escarpment, then down into the valley.

6 KANGAROO VALLEY

This lush, green valley is famous for its dairy farming and is surrounded by the dramatic escarpment over which you have just driven. The old township has some interesting buildings and many tea-shops and cafés.
Continue through the valley and turn left on to the Berry road when you reach the Princes Highway. Follow this road to Kiama.

7 KIAMA

This drive through pleasant rural scenery takes you just off the highway to the seaside town of Kiama. Discovered in 1797 and originally a fishing port, Kiama is now a popular tourist resort with attractive beaches and a famous ocean blowhole. Commercial fishing, although on a small scale, still takes place here.
Return to the highway and continue north to Wollongong.

8 WOLLONGONG

From Kiama, the highway curves inland and follows the shores of Lake Illawarra. This large lake is popular with boating and fishing enthusiasts and provides a recreational centre for the Wollongong/ Port Kembla urban area. Wollongong, 82km south of Sydney, is NSW's third largest city and best known as a port, steelworks and industrial centre.
The area has some excellent beaches, however, and the pleasant city centre is worth a visit.
From Wollongong, continue along the Princes Highway to Thirroul, then turn right on to Lawrence Hargrave Drive.

9 COASTAL SCENIC DRIVE

This road follows the beautiful coastline north of Wollongong. There are several well-marked lookouts along the cliffs, and at Stanwell Park you are quite likely to see hang gliders hovering over the clifftop and beaches below.
From Stanwell Park, return to the Princes Highway, which takes you back to Sydney alongside the Royal National Park.

Beaches

*S*ydney's waterside location has pro-vided the city with a wide choice of beaches, both on the harbour and the ocean, and a large number of these are very close to the city centre.

Enjoying Bondi Beach

Visitors will enjoy Sydney's marvellous beach life, but there are a few things to be aware of. Water pollution has become a problem in recent years, so pay attention to any notices advising against swimming. Other signs to watch out for are the red and yellow flags on ocean beaches. These indicate the stretch of water in which it is safe to swim – if you ignore these, there is a fair chance that you will be swept out to sea and need rescuing! Other marine hazards include sharks (but sightings are rare these days), and jellyfish or marine stingers. Again, warnings are given if the water is considered unsafe.

If you are enjoying a day in the sun, make sure that you wear a hat and apply sunscreen – factor 15 is recommended – liberally. The sun in Sydney is extremely fierce and it is all too easy for visitors to regret their day on the beach. Cover up and develop your tan slowly.

Balmoral
This northside harbour beach is one of Sydney's most attractive bays. Beach swimming is safe here and there is also a pool: Balmoral is a particularly good beach for children. To the right of the bay, located on Middle Head, is HMAS *Penguin* naval base.
Ferry from Circular Quay to Taronga Zoo, then bus 238.

Bondi
Undoubtedly Australia's most famous beach, and the centre of a long tradition of surf activities. During the summer months visitors are likely to witness surf carnivals, which are great entertainment. Apart from the attractions of its sand and surf, Bondi has a slightly run-down seaside town atmosphere, with lots of excellent places to eat, drink, take in the views and shop. The beach pavilion often holds events such as music festivals and exhibitions, and the more energetic will enjoy a coastal path walk from Bondi to Bronte (see pages 30–1).
Train to Bondi Junction, and bus 380.

Bronte
To the south of Bondi, Bronte has an ocean pool and a large picnic area, and is very popular with families.
Train to Bondi Junction, and bus 378.

Coogee
Coogee Bay is a large surfing and family beach, surrounded by a substantial

shopping centre with several pubs and a range of places to eat.
Buses 373/4 from Circular Quay.

Manly

Manly is just a short Jetcat ride across the harbour from the city, and has Sydney's best seaside town atmosphere. There is an excellent, long surf beach, traditional fish and chip shops, and amusements such as the Manly Oceanarium and Manly Pier funfair. From the main beach it is easy to walk to nearby Fairy Bower and Shelly beaches, or, for the more energetic, continue up to North Head for some marvellous views (see page 34-5).
Jetcat or ferry from Circular Quay.

Nielsen Park

The south side's favourite harbour beach is actually called Shark Bay, but don't worry – the beach is protected by a shark-proof net. This lovely little bay provides safe swimming and is surrounded by Nielsen Park, a segment of the Sydney Harbour National Park.

One of the famous Bondi Beach lifeguards

Manly Beach has great surf

This area behind and above the beach is wonderful for picnics. The park also contains a kiosk-style restaurant which serves good food.
Bus 325 from Circular Quay.

Tamarama

Bondi's smaller neighbour is popular with the youthful, body beautiful crowd. It is an attractive little beach, but beware of the often treacherous currents.
Train to Bondi Junction, then bus 391.

FURTHER AFIELD

In addition to these inner city waterside playgrounds, Sydney's north and south sides are blessed with more sandy bays and beaches which the visitor might like to visit.

Northern Beaches

There are a dozen beautiful surf beaches stretching from Manly north to Palm Beach (see pages 36–7).

Southern Beaches

Maroubra and Cronulla are other popular surf beaches within the southern city limits.

Beach Life

Despite gloomy warnings of skin cancer and other, less damaging, effects of the intense Australian sun, Sydneysiders cannot resist a day on the beach. Summer, which can stretch from November to March, presents almost unlimited opportunities for locals of all shapes, ages, sizes and ethnic backgrounds to head for sand, sun and surf at one of the city's many beaches.

Some, especially those who are blessed with a body beautiful, are after a tan and dress accordingly – beachwear for males and females is scanty, to say the least. Ironically, in this domain of under -dressing, beachwear design has become a virtual art-form in Australia. Others head for one of the city's nude beaches for the all-over bronzed look. Many just want to get away from

Out of the water, there's jogging…

… or more acrobatic pastimes

the heat and humidity, and take to the water with an audible sense of relief.

But there is a more important aspect of Sydney beach life – an entire sub-culture lies out there on those golden sands. The visitor's images and expectations will be fulfilled: they really do exist, those muscled, tanned, bleach-maned lifeguards; and those boys and girls who ride the waves with the balance and skill that only comes from many waterlogged hours in the surf.

The beach is a way of life – a place to meet, eat, drink and parade. A place to practise your surfing, kayaking or windsurfing. A place to relax, read, soak up the sun and forget the week's worries. Whatever the motivation, Sydneysiders have turned beach life into a lifestyle of relaxation and hedonism that is perhaps without equal anywhere in the world!

There's plenty to do in or out of the water

Surfing is practically the national sport

Some prefer traditional sunbathing

City Centre

*S*ydney's modern city centre is a mass of high-rise concrete, steel and glass, much of which has, unfortunately, been erected at the expense of older buildings. Among these futuristic structures, however, small pockets of history remain, and these are the most interesting highlights for the visitor.

The Archibald Fountain in Hyde Park

DAVID JONES' DEPARTMENT STORE

This 1927 building houses not just Sydney's finest department store, affectionately known as DJ's, but a glittering array of glass, marble and chrome counters and creations, in what has been described as: 'The most beautiful store in the world'. Uniformed doormen and live grand piano music add to the elegant atmosphere.
Corner of Castlereagh, Market and Elizabeth Streets. Open: during normal shopping hours. Train to St James (City Circle line).

HYDE PARK

Just across the road from DJ's lies the expanse of Hyde Park. The area was declared public land by Governor Phillip in 1792 and became a park in 1810. The formal gardens include fountains and walkways and the park is popular with office workers, particularly at lunchtimes. The southern end (between Park and Liverpool Streets) contains the Anzac War Memorial and Pool of Remembrance. *Between College and Elizabeth Streets.*

MARTIN PLACE

The city's largest plaza stretches east to west from Macquarie to George Streets, and is a popular venue for outdoor lunch-time concerts (weekdays from noon to 2pm). Martin Place is flanked by offices and shopping centres and exhibits an interesting range of architectural styles – from 1990s glass and steel to the sandstone General Post Office of 1874.

QUEEN VICTORIA BUILDING

This vast building, completed in 1898, takes up an entire city block and was constructed to celebrate Queen Victoria's golden jubilee. The 'QVB' originally housed markets and offices, but restoration during the 1980s has transformed the building into Sydney's most beautiful shopping complex. The stained-glass windows and tiled floors are particularly noteworthy.

George Street (between Market and Druitt Streets). Open: daily. Train or bus to Town Hall Station.

ST ANDREWS CATHEDRAL

Near by is Sydney's Anglican cathedral. Construction began in 1837 and the cathedral was consecrated in 1868. The perpendicular gothic structure is built of local sandstone and was designed by the colony's most famous church architect, Edmund Blacket.
Sydney Square, George Street. Open: daily. Bus or train to Town Hall Station.

ST MARY'S CATHEDRAL

The city's Roman Catholic cathedral lies across Hyde Park from David Jones'. Built in the gothic-revival style between 1868 and 1882, the cathedral features an impressive interior with beautiful stained-glass windows. The Australian Museum (see page 62) is located near by.
College Street. Open: daily. Train to St James (City Circle line).

SYDNEY TOWER

This is a must for all visitors. The 305m high tower was completed in 1981 and is

The older style of St Mary's Cathedral

The gleaming modern spire of Sydney Tower

Sydney's most distinctive landmark. A high-speed lift takes you to the observation tower – and astounding views. From here, it's easy to understand the city's layout and take in the marvellous panorama of the harbour. You can also see Botany Bay to the south, and even as far as the Blue Mountains – about 90km away. The view at night is also breathtaking and is best enjoyed by dining in one of the tower's two revolving restaurants.
Centrepoint, Market Street. Open: Monday to Saturday 9.30am–9.30pm; Sundays and holidays 10.30am–6.30pm. Admission fee.

SYDNEY TOWN HALL

Located between the QVB and St Andrew's Cathedral, Sydney Town Hall is an elaborate, sandstone Victorian building which was begun in 1868. It houses council offices and a number of halls, where free musical concerts are often held.
Sydney Square, George Street. Open: Monday to Friday 9am–5pm. Train or bus to Town Hall.

Darling Harbour

Not so long ago, Darling Harbour was a rundown and neglected port wasteland on the western side of the city. However, millions of dollars and several years of reconstruction during the 1980s have transformed the area into one of the city's most attractive precincts. The 50-hectare complex contains a convention centre and exhibition halls, parks, museums, many restaurants and a large shopping mall. Free outdoor entertainment is provided at weekends. The easiest access is by the Monorail from Pitt Street, or it's just a short walk across Pyrmont Bridge from the city centre. For further information on any Darling Harbour attraction, call the Hotline on 0055 20261.

CHINATOWN

Although not essentially a part of Darling Harbour, this interesting ethnic section of the city is close by. The area around Dixon, Hay and Sussex Streets is full of the fascinating shops, stalls and restaurants of Sydney's large Chinese community. The restaurants here are cheap and serve excellent, authentic food. *Monorail to the Haymarket.*

CHINESE GARDEN

This attractive garden is near the Chinatown entrance to Darling Harbour.

The neon glow of Darling Harbour by night

It was designed by landscape architects from China and features typically Cantonese pagodas, bridges and lakes. *Tel: 281 6863. Open: 9.30am–sunset daily. Admission fee. Monorail to the Haymarket.*

HARBOURSIDE

This attractively designed glass and steel centre is one of the city's most likeable examples of modern architecture. The large complex contains dozens of shops, market stalls and eating places. Some of Sydney's most pleasant outdoor eateries are located here, at the waterside. *Open: Sunday to Wednesday 10am–7pm; Thursday to Saturday 10am–9pm.*

THE *JAMES CRAIG* AND *KANANGRA*

Darling Harbour is home to two of Sydney's most historic ships, which are open to the public. The *Kanangra* is a restored 1912 Sydney Harbour ferry, which is painted in bright fairground colours, while the *James Craig* (1874) once plied the waters as a three-masted barque. It is currently a hulk, but is gradually being restored to its former glory. *Tel: 281 9411. Open: daily 10am–5pm. Admission fee.*

Darling Harbour has even more to offer: other major attractions include the Australian National Maritime Museum, the Powerhouse Museum (see pages 62–3), and the Sydney Aquarium (see page 155).

The monorail and the award-winning Powerhouse Museum

MONORAIL

The privately operated Monorail is a controversial 1980s addition to the city's transport system – controversial in the sense that its usefulness (limited) is outweighed by its ugliness (severe). It is, however, the most direct means of travel to Darling Harbour – the most central city station is on Pitt Street, near the corner of Pitt and Market. The raised track then runs in a loop around Darling Harbour and returns to the city.
Open: daily from 7.30am–9pm (to 11pm on Friday and Saturday).

PUMPHOUSE TAVERN

Now a popular and thriving tavern, this three-storey, Italianate building at the Chinatown end of Darling Harbour once contained a hydraulically powered pumphouse. It was completed in 1891.
Pier Street, Haymarket. Open: daily during hotel hours. Monorail to the Haymarket.

PYRMONT BRIDGE

The present bridge replaced the 1858 wooden original, and was opened in 1902 – it features a central panel which opens to allow tall-masted ships access to Darling Harbour. The bridge is now for pedestrians only and is the main walking route to the complex. The fish markets in the area are well worth a visit.
Access from Market Street.

SYDNEY ENTERTAINMENT CENTRE

Completed in 1982, the Entertainment Centre is the city's major venue for rock concerts, musical events and indoor sports such as basketball and tennis. The large complex can hold up to 12,000 people. For further information on entertainment in Sydney, see pages 148 to 155.
Corner of Hay and Harbour Streets. Monorail to the Haymarket.

Multi-cultural Sydney

Any visitor will soon realise that Sydney is a truly multi-cultural city. There is still an abundance of those stereotyped and unmistakably Anglo-Saxon blonde, tanned beach girls and boys, but the times are certainly changing. A walk through city streets, or a ride on a metropolitan train or bus, reveals a very different picture.

Since World War II, Australia's immigration policy has gone through phases varying from an open-armed welcome to a definitely cold shoulder, but there have been distinct waves of immigration. The post-war influx of Europeans – including Hungarians, Yugoslavs, Turks, Greeks and Italians – was succeeded during the 1970s and '80s by a tide of Lebanese and Asians. The Vietnamese and Cambodians also came as refugees from their ravaged and war-torn homelands.

The 1980s saw a different picture, as South Africans and prosperous Hong Kong residents escaped their home country problems for a new life in Australia. There are always the inevitable British arrivals, as well as a large community of New Zealanders, Maoris and Pacific Islanders. Nowadays, Aborigines make up only a small proportion of the city's population.

Most of these immigrants aimed for Sydney, and the result is a community that is colourfully diverse, and generally racially harmonious. In Sydney it is not uncommon to see signs in four languages, and the city's White Pages telephone book lists Community Interpreter Services for 23 languages from English to Khmer; Croatian to Thai; and Italian to Arabic.

Around 70 per cent of Sydney's population has at least two different ethnic backgrounds. Out on the street, this means an incredible diversity of faces, accents and languages, as well as a wonderful range of shops, and restaurants serving a multitude of cuisines. It all contributes to the city's vibrant atmosphere.

...and are attracted by the quality of life

Traditional customs carry over to modern life

Immigrants are drawn to the beauty of their adopted land...

Sydneysiders accustom themselves to a rich variety of languages

The Domain and the Royal Botanic Gardens

*T*his large reserve of gardens and greenery, bordered by Macquarie Street, Farm Cove and Woolloomooloo Bay, is one of Sydney's most delightful enclaves, and a favourite recreation area for Sydneysiders. The 70-hectare area is now divided into two parts by the Cahill Expressway, but was laid out in 1810 as the domain of the Governor of New South Wales. It is an easy walk to this area from the city centre, or take the Sydney Explorer Bus which travels along Art Gallery Road to Mrs Macquarie's Point and passes the Royal Botanic Gardens entrance. Free bus no 666 from the city centre stops outside the Art Gallery.

THE DOMAIN
The Domain forms the southern section of this peaceful inner-city haven, but also extends alongside the Botanic Gardens to Mrs Macquarie's Point, which stretches out to form the eastern boundary of Farm Cove.

This grassy area is bordered by huge Moreton Bay fig trees and is popular with lunchtime joggers and office workers. On Sunday mornings the area near the Art Gallery becomes Sydney's 'Speakers' Corner', where you can listen to discussions of topics ranging from politics to AIDS. In January each year, open-air opera and symphony concerts, which attract many thousands of people, are held in the Domain.

Art Gallery of New South Wales
The Domain contains the state's premier art gallery, a must for visitors (see page 54).

Andrew 'Boy' Charlton Pool
This harbourside public swimming pool is open from October to June and is a magnet for office workers at lunchtimes and after work. The present pool dates from 1966 and is named after a 1920s Australian swimming champion.
Mrs Macquarie's Road, The Domain. Tel: 358 6686. Open: daily from 7am. There is a small admission fee.

Mrs Macquarie's Point
Named after the wife of Governor Macquarie, this vantage point provides excellent views of the Opera House, Harbour Bridge, north shore and the eastern part of the harbour. The point features Mrs Macquarie's Chair (see page 23).

The Royal Botanic Gardens

Woolloomooloo Bay

This deeply indented bay forms the eastern boundary of the Domain and features the historic 'Finger Wharf', which was long used as the embarkation point for long distance ocean travellers. The far side of the bay is the Fleet Base for ships of the Royal Australian Navy.

ROYAL BOTANIC GARDENS

Sydney's premier gardens surround the broad sweep of Farm Cove, where convicts, under the orders of Governor Phillip, established the Government Farm soon after the arrival of the First Fleet in 1788. The Botanic Gardens were founded in 1816 and greatly expanded in the period up to 1831. Today's 30 hectares contain a marvellous display of native Australian plants such as eucalypts, rainforest flora and bottlebrush, as well as plants and trees from southeast Asia, Africa and the Pacific.

Special features of the gardens include the National Herbarium, which was established in 1985 to study native plant species. The centre also contains some of the first plants (dried for preservation) collected by Cook's companion, Sir Joseph Banks, at Botany Bay in 1770. The Sydney Tropical Centre is housed in two futuristic buildings, the Arc and the Pyramid Glasshouse, and features a living display of tropical ecosystems.

Visitor Centre and Gardens Restaurant

The centre includes a book and gift shop, displays on the gardens, and leaflets which describe self-guided walks. Free guided walks of the gardens depart from the Visitor Centre at 10am on Wednesdays and Fridays, and on Sundays at 1pm. Near by, the excellent Gardens Restaurant is open for lunch and afternoon teas daily.

Domain Pool, Woolloomooloo Bay

Entrance from Mrs Macquarie's Road. Tel: 231 8125. Open: daily 9am–5pm; Arc and Pyramid glasshouses 10am–6pm (summer), 10am–4pm (rest of year). Admission free.

Farm Cove

Prior to British settlement in 1788, Farm Cove was a sacred initiation site belonging to one of the area's Aboriginal tribes. From 1848 to 1878 a sea wall was built around the cove to retain and reclaim the swampy foreshore.

Government House

The official residence of the Governor of New South Wales is located on a hill on the western side of the Botanic Gardens. The mansion dates from 1845 and is built of local stone in the gothic-revival style. Unfortunately, Government House is open to the public only on special occasions.

Galleries

*S*ydney's art galleries offer the visitor a special opportunity to view and appreciate two uniquely Australian forms of art. Aboriginal works represent one of the world's most fascinating forms of decorative art, while Australian 19th- and 20th-century paintings are particularly appealing for their use of colour, light and unmistakably Australian subject matter. In addition, the exciting new Museum of Contemporary Art has added another dimension to Sydney's art scene.

ABORIGINAL ARTISTS GALLERY

Although this is a commercial gallery, it provides one of the best opportunities to view contemporary Aboriginal and Islander art. The gallery was established by the Australian Government and displays bark paintings, prints, weavings, didgeridoos, carvings and other decorated artefacts.
Civic House, 477 Kent Street, City (behind Town Hall). Tel: 261 2929. Open: Monday to Saturday 9am–5.30pm. Free admission. Train to Town Hall Station.

ART GALLERY OF NEW SOUTH WALES

The AGNSW is located in a large Victorian building, with several modern extensions, in a fine position opposite the Domain. The gallery consists of a large permanent collection, but also features changing exhibitions of an international standard. The emphasis is on Australian art, with the 19th-century collection being of particular interest. Many works of Tom Roberts, Elioth Gruner, Arthur Streeton and other

The Art Gallery of New South Wales – emphasis on Australian art and local artists

artists of the period are featured. There is also a good range of European and photographic art, contemporary works, and an excellent Aboriginal display in the basement. The gallery has a comprehensive bookshop which sells prints and cards, and a better than average restaurant and café.
Art Gallery Road, The Domain. Tel: 225 1700. Open: Monday to Saturday 10am–5pm; Sunday noon–5pm. Free admission, with an entrance fee for special exhibitions. Sydney Explorer Bus, or free bus 666 from the city centre.

The S H Ervin is a must for art-lovers

S H ERVIN GALLERY

The S H Ervin is one of Sydney's largest non-commercial galleries and is housed in the National Trust Centre on Observatory Hill – the building dates from 1815 and was originally a military hospital.

The gallery opened in 1978 and features changing exhibitions – these have included works by famed Australian artists Hans Heysen, Conrad Martens, Russell Drysdale and Lloyd Rees. Other exhibitions focus on Australian history, or regional themes such as Sydney Harbour and the Blue Mountains. The centre includes a bookstore and excellent tea-rooms. You can combine an

excursion to the gallery with visits to the nearby Observatory and Millers Point.
National Trust Centre, Observatory Hill, The Rocks. Tel: 258 0174. Open: Tuesday to Friday 11am–5pm; Saturday and Sunday noon–5pm. Admission fee. Bus 431 or 433 to Millers Point, or Sydney Explorer Bus.

MUSEUM OF CONTEMPORARY ART

Sydney's newest art gallery was once the Maritime Services Board offices, but opened at the end of 1991 as Australia's first major museum for international contemporary arts. The innovative art deco-style museum houses the fine Dr J W Power collection of 4,500 paintings, sculptures and other pieces of visual art, and also features changing international exhibitions. The excellent café has magnificent views of the Opera House and the museum's shop is ideal for purchasing unusual books, posters and other gifts.
132 George Street, Circular Quay West, City. Tel: 252 4033. Open: daily except Tuesday 11am–7pm. Admission fee. Bus or train to Circular Quay.

COMMERCIAL GALLERIES

The suburbs of Paddington and Woollahra contain many commercial galleries which specialise in contemporary Australian art. Two of the best are:

Barry Stern Galleries
19-21 Glenmore Road, Paddington. Tel: 331 4676. Open: Monday to Saturday 11.30am–5.30pm.

Holdsworth Galleries
86 Holdsworth Street, Woollahra. Tel: 363 1364. Open: Monday to Saturday 10am–5pm; Sunday noon–5pm.

Historic Houses

Sydney's short European history, and the city's apparent penchant for demolishing, rebuilding and demolishing yet again, means that there are few remaining historic houses. But although limited in number, the surviving 19th-century dwellings are certainly worth visiting.

The suburb of Parramatta, Australia's second oldest settlement, contains three more historic homes (see pages 92–3 and also Paddington on pages 88–89).

The ex-convict John Cadman's house

CADMAN'S COTTAGE

Built in 1816 as a barracks for Governor Macquarie's boat crew, Cadman's Cottage is the oldest surviving house in the city of Sydney. The small two-storey cottage is constructed of sandstone and was named after ex-convict John Cadman, the government coxswain of the time. He lived here until 1854. The building has housed the Sydney Water Police and was once part of a sailors' home, but has been restored and now contains a National Parks and Wildlife Service information centre and shop.
110 George Street, The Rocks.
Tel: 247 8861. Open: Monday to Friday 9am–4.30pm; Saturday and Sunday 11am–4pm. No admission fee. Bus or train to Circular Quay.

ELIZABETH BAY HOUSE

Regarded in its day as the colony's finest residence, Elizabeth Bay House was designed by John Verge, the most fashionable architect and builder of the 1830s. The two-storey Regency house was constructed from 1835 onwards for the Colonial Secretary, Alexander Macleay and focuses on a central oval saloon with a winding staircase and domed ceiling. It occupies a fine position overlooking the harbour, to where its landscaped grounds once stretched: the area now contains a park and many old-style apartment buildings. This elegant mansion is furnished in the style of the 1840s and often features exhibitions in the upstairs rooms. Free guided tours are included in the admission charge (see page 84).
7 Onslow Avenue, Elizabeth Bay.
Tel: 358 2344. Open: Tuesday to Sunday 10am–4.30pm. Admission fee. Sydney Explorer Bus, or train to Kings Cross.

THE ROCKS

The Rocks, Sydney's oldest suburb, contains many houses and hotels dating from the mid- and late 19th century. Lower Fort Street, from Argyle Place to

Dawes Point, has the city's best examples of Colonial Georgian (1830s) and Regency houses, while George Street contains several buildings from the 1880s. Examples are the Russell Hotel, 143 George Street (1887); the Old Police Station, 127 George Street (1882); and Sergeant-Major's Row, behind 29–41 George Street (1881–83). Further information and detailed pictorial maps of the area are available from The Rocks Visitor Centre at 104 George Street.

Bus or train to Circular Quay, or Sydney Explorer Bus.

VAUCLUSE HOUSE

This gothic mansion is set in 11 hectares of gardens, bushland and beach frontage on Sydney Harbour: the house dates from 1803, but most of the construction took place in the 1830s. Vaucluse House was the home of William Charles Wentworth, barrister, explorer and 'Father of the Australian Constitution'. The 15 rooms include a lavishly decorated suite for entertaining and are furnished in the style of the mid-19th century. The delightful gardens are perfect for a picnic, and the house also contains excellent tea-rooms.

Wentworth Road, Vaucluse. Tel: 337 1957. Open: Tuesday to Sunday 10am–4.30pm. Admission fee. Bus 325 from Circular Quay.

VIENNA COTTAGE

This fine example of a small, stone tradesman's cottage was built by shoemaker John Hellman in 1871, in harbourside Hunters Hill, now an expensive and fashionable Sydney suburb. The cottage is interesting both for its architecture and displays on the history of the area. The ferry trip to Hunters Hill is enjoyable, as is a wander around the suburb.

38 Alexandra Street, Hunters Hill. Tel: 817 2240. Open: Saturday 2pm–4pm; Sunday 11am–4pm. Admission fee. Ferry from Circular Quay to Valentia Street Wharf.

The colonial elegance of Vaucluse House

Sydney's Architecture

Traditional family homes in the Kirribilli area

Exquisi lacework balconies the Baysw district

Typical rural architecture in NSW

The pristine brilliance of Macquarie lighthouse

Visitors to Sydney are always enchanted by the city's lovely colonial architecture. A walk along Macquarie Street, in particular, reveals some of the very best examples. The clean lines of Francis Greenway's Georgian Hyde Park Barracks are complemented by the simple, verandahed State Parliament House, just a few metres away.

Architectural concepts, like most of the imported British ideas and standards of the early settlers, became adapted to the antipodean climate and lifestyle. Cottages may have been built along English lines, but cooling verandahs were added to combat the summer heat. In Paddington, the idea of the balcony was attractively developed. A stroll through this historic suburb reveals the city's most pleasing architecture – not in grand mansions, but in the decorative iron lacework fences and balcony railings of ordinary workers' cottages of the 1850s to 1890s.

The genius of Francis Greenway

Sydney's finest colonial buildings are a tribute to the genius of Francis Greenway (1777–1837), a skilled architect who was transported in 1813 for forgery. The fledgling colony was fortunate that he was spared the death penalty and sent instead to Botany Bay.

Greenway was pardoned, and appointed civil architect by Governor Macquarie in 1816. With his new-found liberty he set about transforming the ramshackle city. Macquarie Street contains three of his most celebrated Colonial Georgian buildings – the 1819 Hyde Park Barracks, St James' Church (1822) and the Supreme Court (1828), as well as his gothic-style Conservatorium of Music (1819).

Other Greenway gems that follow his harmoniously proportioned Georgian lines include the Macquarie Lighthouse at South Head (1817) and buildings at Windsor – the Court House (1822) and St Matthew's Church (1820).

Delightful residence near Newcastle

Macquarie Street

*I*n a city with an apparent dedication to the controversial merits of modern architecture, it is fortunate that Macquarie Street and its fine buildings have been spared the developers' bulldozers.

Macquarie Street began life, as did most of the city's roads, as a narrow cart-track leading away from Sydney Cove. In 1810, however, Governor Lachlan Macquarie began to remodel the thoroughfare and ultimately created Sydney's most stylish street. It contains some of the city's most important buildings, both in function and architectural interest.

The Sydney Explorer Bus travels along Macquarie Street, or you can catch a train to Martin Place.

HYDE PARK BARRACKS

This classic Georgian-style building, designed by the important 19th-century architect Francis Greenway, is now one of Sydney's leading museums (see page 63).

The Mint – now a museum of decorative art

THE MINT

Next door to the Barracks, the Mint was built in 1816 as a section of the famous 'Rum Hospital', but later became the first branch of the Royal Mint outside of London. Gold coins were produced here from 1851 to 1927. The building is in Colonial Georgian style and has a simple two-storey façade, surrounded by colonnaded verandahs. In 1982 The Mint opened, after extensive restoration, as a museum of the decorative arts. The collection includes gold coins, stamps and furniture.
Corner of Queen's Square and Macquarie Street. Tel: 217 0333. Open: daily (except Wednesday) 10am–5pm, Wednesday noon–5pm. Free admission.

NEW SOUTH WALES STATE CONSERVATORIUM OF MUSIC

Adjoining the Botanic Gardens, at the northern end of Macquarie Street, the 1819 gothic 'fortress'-style Conservatorium was designed by Francis Greenway, but represents a striking departure from his usual clean lines. The building was originally the governor's stable and offices.
Conservatorium Road, off Macquarie Street. Tel: 230 1222. Open: daily 9am–4pm. Free admission.

QUEEN'S SQUARE

The southern end of Macquarie Street terminates at Queen's Square, named after the 1888 statue of Queen Victoria. Across the road, outside the Hyde Park Barracks, stands a statue of Prince Albert, dating from 1866.

ST JAMES CHURCH
The city's oldest church is a graceful Francis Greenway design which dates from 1822. This brick Colonial Georgian building is topped by a spire which, although now lost among the high-rise office blocks, once served as a landmark for ships entering Sydney Harbour.
Queen's Square. Open: Monday to Friday 8am–5pm, Saturday 8am–6pm, Sunday 8am–4pm. Free admission.

STATE LIBRARY OF NEW SOUTH WALES
The library contains a vast collection of books and other material on Australia and the Pacific region. It is housed both in the 1910 Mitchell Wing, and in a modern concrete and glass addition. The library often holds exhibitions with Australian themes; films are also screened regularly.
Corner of Macquarie Street and Shakespeare Place. Tel: 230 1414. Open: Monday to Friday 9am–9pm, Saturday 9am–5pm, Sunday 11am–5pm. Free admission.

STATE PARLIAMENT HOUSE
This attractive verandahed building has been the seat of state government since 1827. The simple structure dates from 1810 to 1816 and was originally a wing of the Rum Hospital. Interested visitors are allowed to watch Parliament in session.
Macquarie Street. Tel: 230 2111 for session bookings. Open: Monday to Friday 9.30am–4pm. Free admission.

Having a break outside Hyde Park Barracks

SYDNEY HOSPITAL
The current Victorian sandstone hospital buildings were completed in 1894 and replaced the main block of the Rum Hospital. Outside the hospital, on Macquarie Street, is a replica of the famous Florentine statue *Il Porcellino* (wild boar).

THE RUM HOSPITAL
It is an interesting quirk of Sydney's history that its first hospital was built on the proceeds of rum consumption – in the early days, rum was the virtual currency of the colony. In 1811 Governor Macquarie awarded a share in an extremely lucrative monopoly on the importation of rum to D'Arcy Wentworth, the Surgeon-in-Charge – in exchange for the building of the city's general hospital. Convicts were employed in its construction and it was completed in 1816. Today, all that remains of the original hospital is State Parliament House, the old north block, and The Mint (south wing).

Museums

*S*ydney's museums provide the visitor with a fascinating insight into Australia's geological, Aboriginal, colonial, maritime and technological histories. The Australian Museum and the Powerhouse are particularly recommended.

AUSTRALIAN MUSEUM

The excellent Australian Museum contains the country's largest display of ethnographic and natural history displays – it is rated as one of the world's best in its field. The building dates from 1849, but has been greatly expanded over the years to house the varied displays. Museum highlights include an illuminating Aboriginal historical and cultural display; a mammals gallery featuring Australia's unique wildlife, and a section covering cultures of the Pacific

The Australian Museum is a popular venue

Islands. Free guided tours are available.
6 College Street, City. Tel: 339 8111.
Open: daily 10am–5pm. Admission fee.
Train to Museum Station.

AUSTRALIAN NATIONAL MARITIME MUSEUM

This new museum, opened in 1991, is dedicated to Australia's maritime history and features a large range of both indoor and outdoor exhibits: the latter are moored at the museum's wharves. Displays include the famous *Australia II*, the yacht which won the America's Cup for Australia in 1983, and the sternpost

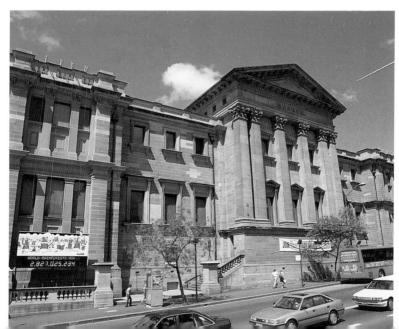

of Captain Cook's *Endeavour*. Other exhibits feature displays on the navy, the discovery of the continent, the history of commercial fishing and whaling and the voyages of the many migrants who have arrived in Australia by sea.
Darling Harbour. Tel: 552 7777. Open: daily 10am–5pm. Admission fee. Monorail to Darling Harbour.

EARTH EXCHANGE

Sydney's old geological and mining museum has been transformed into a three-level series of exciting, interactive exhibits. The displays include a simulated earthquake and a Hawaiian volcano, Aboriginal art and legends, environmental features, and the country's best mineral collection. The complex also houses a specialist gem shop, the Minerals and Energy Information Centre and a café/restaurant with views of the Opera House and harbour (see pages 24-5).
18 Hickson Road, The Rocks. Tel: 251 2422. Open: daily 10am–5pm. Admission fee. Sydney Explorer bus.

HYDE PARK BARRACKS

The historic Barracks building is as interesting as its contents. Designed by convict architect Francis Greenway, this Georgian-style, three-storey brick construction was built in 1819 to house convicts. The building has had many uses, including a period as a lodging house for destitute women. Renovations began in 1979 and the Barracks now contains a museum devoted to the early history of the colony.
Queen's Square, Macquarie Street. Tel: 217 0111. Open: daily (except Tuesday morning) 10am–5pm. Free admission. Train to St James' or Martin Place.

Inside the Powerhouse Museum

POWERHOUSE MUSEUM

This award-winning museum is housed in an 1899 power station and contains the bulk of the Museum of Applied Arts and Sciences' vast collection. Exhibits range from the decorative arts and social history to science and technology and are spread throughout the vast engine and boiler houses of the old power station. The museum is fun for all, but children in particular will enjoy the many educational hands-on displays which encourage participation.
500 Harris Street, Ultimo. Tel: 217 0100. Open: daily 10am–5pm. Admission fee. Monorail to the Haymarket.

OTHER MUSEUMS

Two other museums are featured elsewhere: the Museum of Australian Childhood (see page 154), and the Sydney Tramway Museum (see page 107).

The Rocks

*F*lanking Sydney Cove, opposite the Opera House, lies The Rocks – the oldest 'village' in Sydney, and indeed Australia. It was here on this rocky sandstone area that the first convict tents were pitched when the First Fleet arrived in 1788. The Rocks later became the site of the colony's first hospital, fort, windmill, bakery and wharves, and during the 19th century the area developed into the heart of Sydney's trade and commerce. Fortunately, despite a turbulent history, many of the buildings of this era remain and today The Rocks is the city's premier tourist destination. There is a great deal to see here, and a full day should be put aside for exploration. You may even want to return again – and again!

The Rocks Visitor Centre at 104 George Street should be a priority. The Centre provides excellent information and maps of the area, and also conducts walking tours.

Access to The Rocks is by train or bus to Circular Quay, or via the Sydney Explorer Bus. Once in this compact area, it is essential to walk to really

George Street is the heart of The Rocks

appreciate the harbour vistas, historic buildings and streets (see pages 24-5).

GEORGE STREET

Australia's oldest street was originally a cart-track leading to The Rocks from the city's major water supply, the Tank Stream. It was initially called Spring Row, but became George Street in 1810 in honour of King George III. The original tents of 1788 were gradually

replaced by rough wattle and daub huts, and these in turn were superseded by more substantial structures – many of which still remain. The entire street, from Circular Quay to Dawes Point, is of historical value, as a walk through the area will reveal.

HARRINGTON STREET

This is another interesting thoroughfare, running off Argyle Street. It contains the excellent Gumnut Tea Garden, which is housed in Reynolds Cottage – a two-storey rubble and stone house built in 1830 by William Reynolds, an Irish blacksmith.

NURSES' WALK AND SUEZ CANAL

These interesting narrow lanes run off Harrington Street: both have been restored and contain some interesting shops and galleries. They look attractive today, but in the 1870s such streets were crowded, unsanitary and the haunt of the notorious Rocks thieves and pickpockets.

A colourful history

Walking around the beautifully restored Rocks area today, it is hard to imagine what it once looked like. This small suburb that was the birthplace of the nation has been the scene of a colourful, turbulent and often violent history.

In the earliest days, the convicts' tents were erected here, well away from the officers and gentlemen who chose the opposite side of Sydney Cove as their enclave. As Sydney developed into a port for lawless whalers and sealers during the early 19th century, The Rocks became crowded with brothels and inns selling the ubiquitous rum, which had virtually become the colony's currency. Violence

and robbery were the norm in this maze of narrow lanes, overcrowded with people and marred by open sewers and unsanitary conditions.

During the 1850s goldrush era, The Rocks became Sydney's first Chinatown;

Many older buildings were lost when space was cleared for the Cahill Expressway

later years saw the emergence of a true slum in the area and The Rocks 'Pushes' – gangs of thugs armed with razor blades who roamed the city looking for a fight. The bubonic plague outbreak in The Rocks in 1900 killed over 100 people, but turned out to be a blessing in disguise. The rundown huts and shanties were demolished and the area was generally cleaned up. More changes came during the 1920s and 1950s when many Georgian and Victorian houses were removed to make way for the Harbour Bridge approaches and the Cahill Expressway respectively.

Careful restoration during the 1980s has improved The Rocks dramatically and created Sydney's most colourful and fascinating village.

Argyle Street and Observatory Hill

*T*his is the western section of The Rocks, which leads to Miller's Point (see pages 68–9).

ARGYLE STREET

This wide road branches off George Street: on its right-hand side the street is flanked by vast old sandstone warehouses, which have been renovated and converted in recent years.

Argyle Centre

Long used as bond stores and warehouses, this four-storey building dates from 1828. It is now an attractive shopping and restaurant complex, where visitors will find many of their souvenir requirements. Behind the centre lies a row of small Victorian workers' cottages in Playfair Street – see below.

Argyle Cut

Further up the hill, the road passes under a section of the Harbour Bridge on its way to Argyle Place and Miller's Point. This opening in the solid sandstone cliff was hand-cut during the 1840s and 1850s

The sandstone façade of Sydney Observatory

by convicts and, later, free labourers. On the right, immediately before the bridge, are some stairs which lead up to the Harbour Bridge walkway entrance.

Playfair Street and The Rocks Square

Adjacent to the Argyle Centre, The Rocks Square is a pleasant place to sit and watch the free entertainment which is provided at weekends. The square contains an interesting sandstone sculpture – *First Impressions* – which depicts a convict, a soldier and a family of settlers. The old Playfair Street cottages now contain a variety of shops and cafés and are linked with the Argyle Centre.

OBSERVATORY HILL

This is the city's highest point at 44m. It was originally known as Windmill Hill, after a windmill erected here in 1795, and later became the site of a fort: a signal station was added in 1848. Little remains of these structures except wall fragments which now form part of the Observatory. The one-time landmark is now dwarfed by city buildings and the Harbour Bridge, but the view from here is still superb. The hill's park is a great place for a picnic lunch with a 180-degree harbour outlook.
Observatory Hill is reached by Sydney Explorer Bus, or service 431 from George Street.

National Trust Centre

The NSW headquarters of the National

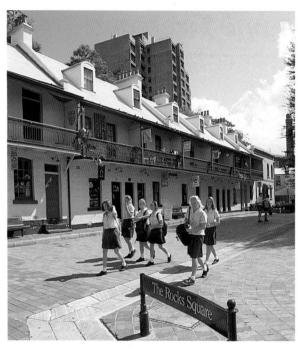

Other major attractions in The Rocks area include Cadman's Cottage, George Street (see pages 56), the Earth Exchange, Sydney's geological and mining museum on Hickson Road (see page 63) and the Museum of Contemporary Art at Circular Quay West (see page 55).

A day out in The Rocks

Trust lie behind Observatory Hill and are housed in a building (1815) which was originally a military hospital built by Governor Macquarie. The centre can provide information on National Trust properties throughout the state and has an excellent gift shop and tea-rooms. The fine S H Ervin Gallery is also housed in the National Trust building (see page 55). *Open (National Trust Centre): Monday to Friday 9am–5pm, weekends 2pm–5pm.*

Sydney Observatory
Established in 1858, the Sydney Observatory was set up to study the southern sky, which was little known at the time. The Italian Renaissance style sandstone buildings include an observatory and time ball tower, but are

no longer used for their original purpose – air pollution and the night lights of the city have made observation of the skies too difficult. The complex of buildings is now a museum of astronomy which children in particular will enjoy. The Observatory is also open in the evenings for a night-time star-gazing session. *Tel: 241 2478. Open: weekdays 2pm–5pm, weekends 10am–5pm. Admission free.*

The Story of Sydney
This multi-media presentation combines a guided tour with theatre, cinema, music and exhibitions to present the history of Australia's first settlement. The complex also contains a café and gift shop. *100 George Street. Tel: 247 7777. Open: daily 10am–5pm. Admission fee.*

Around the Rocks

*A*djacent to The Rocks proper are three interesting scenic areas: Campbell's Cove, Dawes Point and Miller's Point offering refreshing views.

CAMPBELL'S COVE

Just off Hickson Road, which branches off George Street, Campbell's Cove is a delightfully restored precinct of restaurants. These large, gabled, sandstone buildings were constructed between 1838 and 1895 as Campbell's Stores and were used as warehouses for the nearby port.

The area is now a very pleasant place to sit and look out at the harbour and tall ships, such as the *Bounty*, often moor here.

DAWES POINT

Dawes Point, named after the marine and astronomer William Dawes, forms the western limits of Sydney Cove. Lieutenant Dawes established his crude observatory here (originally in a tent) in 1788; later, a battery was erected which commanded the entrance to Sydney Cove. A fort replaced the original battery, but this was demolished in 1924 to make way for the Harbour Bridge pylons.

DAWES POINT RESERVE

Immediately underneath the Sydney Harbour Bridge – of which it gives an unusual perspective – this park also provides excellent views of the harbour itself, the Opera House and the north shore.

WALSH BAY

Walsh Bay, between Dawes Point and

Miller's Point, was once a busy port for whaling and sealing ships and Sydney's first ocean passenger terminal was built here in 1912.

The wharves still stand, but are no longer used for commercial shipping – one of these wooden structures is now the home of the Wharf Theatre and an excellent restaurant.

Access to Dawes Point and Walsh Bay is via Hickson Road in The Rocks.

The Lord Nelson, Sydney's oldest hotel, is still open for business

MILLER'S POINT

The delightful western portion of The Rocks (west of the Harbour Bridge approaches) is known as Miller's Point. This area is reached by the Sydney Explorer Bus, or service 431 from George Street.

ARGYLE PLACE

The historic buildings of this mini-suburb are grouped around attractive Argyle Place – originally known as the Village Green, which was named by Governor Macquarie after his birthplace in Scotland.

GARRISON CHURCH

Located on the eastern side of the green, the small gothic-revival Garrison Church dates from 1840 and is one of Sydney's oldest churches. Although correctly named Holy Trinity Church, the regular attendance of the British Redcoats, who were stationed near by at Dawes Point Battery, led to the nickname which still persists, long after the troops were removed in 1880.

LORD NELSON HOTEL

On the western side of Argyle Place, in Kent Street, is a fine, sandstone, Georgian building which has the honour of being Sydney's oldest hotel and is still in business.

Originally built as a private house in 1834, it became licensed in 1842. The pub has a wonderful atmosphere, with specially brewed beers, and there is an excellent upstairs restaurant.

LOWER FORT STREET

Stretching from Argyle Place to Dawes Point, Lower Fort Street was originally a track which led from the Dawes Point Battery to Observatory Hill, and is one

The oddly-shaped Hero of Waterloo is the city's second oldest hotel, and is a great attraction to visitors

of the city's most interesting thorough-fares. The houses here are a handsome blend of 1830s Colonial Georgian and Regency styles built for the aristocracy, and many of them have been recently restored.

The Hero of Waterloo, situated on the corner of Windmill and Lower Fort streets, was built in 1844 and is the city's second oldest hotel. Along with the Lord Nelson Hotel, it is one of the city's most characterful watering holes and is a great place to soak up the local atmosphere.

Sydney Harbour

*P*ort Jackson, more commonly known as Sydney Harbour, is the essence of the city. From that January day in 1788 when the First Fleet made its tentative path down the waterway, to the gargantuan tankers that ply the sea today, the harbour has been alive with ships bringing people and goods to the Harbour City. But there is more to the harbour than this – the waterway and its distinctive bridge, along with the unmistakable silhouette of the Opera House, are the very symbols of Sydney; people the world over know Sydney from this portrait.

The Harbour Bridge from North Side

SYDNEY HARBOUR

James Cook and his crew on the *Endeavour* passed the entrance to Sydney Harbour in 1770, on their way north from Botany Bay. Although Cook did not investigate further, he noted that: ' . . . there appear'd to be safe Anchorage, which I called Port Jackson'. The name was in honour of Sir George Jackson, Judge-Advocate of the Fleet. It was not until the arrival of the First Fleet in 1788, and their dismay at the barren prospects of Botany Bay, that the waterway was explored. To the delight of Captain Phillip and his weary companions, Port Jackson proved to be a far more suitable location for the new settlement, and on 26 January 1788 the British flag was raised on the shores of Sydney Cove, near the present site of Circular Quay. Tents were erected and this far-flung outpost of Britain began life.

Port Jackson has changed a great deal in the past 200 years. From those first few tents and huts that sprang up at Farm Cove and in The Rocks, Sydney has grown dramatically. The harbour is now busy with maritime traffic and is surrounded by docks and wharves, high-rise office blocks and a multitude of red-roofed dwellings. The 20th century has also seen the construction of two of the city's most famous harbour landmarks: the Harbour Bridge, completed in 1932 and Sydney Opera House, opened in 1973. But, thankfully, large sections of bush and heathland remain and parts of the shore are under the auspices of the Sydney Harbour National Park.

For the tourist, the Harbour is one of the city's most appealing and magnetic attractions. A visit to Sydney is all about the water – riding on ferries and cruise boats, bathing in the harbour waters, and those wonderful views – from lookouts, picnic spots, restaurants, headlands and parks.

The harbour by ferry
Ferry rides are one of the best ways to experience Sydney's aquatic gem. From Circular Quay there is a constant procession of ferries making their way to and from suburbs north, west and east of the bridge. Fares are relatively cheap, and even with no particular destination in mind, visitors will just enjoy being out on the water.

On the north shore you can visit suburbs such as Kirribilli, Neutral Bay, Mosman and Cremorne, or take a cross-harbour trip to Taronga Zoo. The beachside suburb of Manly is accessible either by ferry or the fast Jetcat service. The scenery west of the bridge is completely different – ferry rides to the historic suburbs of Hunters Hill or

Architectural wonder of the modern world

Balmain take you past busy docklands and narrow inlets. At weekends there are also services to Rose Bay and Watsons Bay in the eastern suburbs.

Sydney Ferries operate a variety of reasonably priced harbour cruises which last for around two hours and take in the sights and history of the city's magnificent waterway. There is also an evening Harbour Lights Cruise. For full details of ferry trips telephone 954 4422.

The harbour foreshore
If you just want to amble around the harbour foreshore and take in the views from dry land, there are many scenic walks. The best, and most accessible, is from Dawes Point (under the south side of the Harbour Bridge) to Mrs Macquarie's Point in The Domain. This is a one-hour, easy to follow, stroll which takes in Sydney Cove, Circular Quay, the Opera House and the Botanic Gardens (see pages 22-3).

Sydney Harbour Bridge

*P*rior to the construction of what locals affectionately call the 'Coathanger', the only method of crossing Sydney Harbour was by ferry. In the 1920s and early 1930s there were around 70 steamers ceaselessly plying their way between the city and north shore. As the population increased and the age of the motor car came to stay, this became impractical and work commenced on building a bridge in 1923. It took almost nine years to join the two halves which had sprung up from Dawes Point on the south side, to Milsons Point on the north shore, but the Bridge was finally opened in March 1932.

A view famous the world over

Sydney Harbour Bridge is listed in the *Guinness Book of Records* as the world's widest long-span bridge. The 502.9m span is 48.8m wide and contains eight roadway lanes, two railway tracks, a footpath and a cycleway. The structure contains some 6 million rivets and one coat of paint requires 30,000 litres. Motorists pay a toll when crossing from north to south to help pay for the annual

maintenance costs of around A$3 million. The internationally famous comedian and movie star, Paul Hogan of *Crocodile Dundee* fame, was once a Harbour Bridge painter!

Nowadays, the thoroughfare is a hive of frantic activity that could never have been anticipated in the 1930s, and morning and evening rush hour periods cause increasing delays for frustrated drivers. So much so, that work is under-way on the construction of a tunnel

The Craft Centre in The Rocks

Open: you can visit the Pylon between 10am–5pm daily, from mid-October to mid-February. At other times from Saturday to Tuesday inclusive and public holidays. Admission fee.

HARBOUR ISLANDS
Fort Denison
Sydney's most interesting island, located between Kirribilli Point and Garden Island Naval Base, was long known as 'Pinchgut' – due to the practice of marooning particularly intransigent convicts here, with only ship's biscuits and water to survive on. The rocky island was levelled by convicts during the 1830s and the present fort constructed in 1857, as a precaution against a feared Russian invasion during the Crimean War. The building is now used as a lighthouse by the Maritime Services Board and is perhaps the city's best address!
State Transit ferries visit Fort Denison as part of a harbour cruise. Tel: 954 4422 for details.

Sydney Harbour National Park Islands
Three harbour islands are maintained by the National Parks and Wildlife Service. Shark Island, off Rose Bay, Clark Island, near Darling Point, and Rodd Island, west of the Harbour Bridge, can all be visited, but only by private transport. Shark and Clark are great places for a picnic, and you can hire a water taxi if you are interested in visiting these off-the-beaten-track locations (see page 139).

under the harbour. This is due to open by 1993 and will take a great deal of pressure off the bridge.

Although the Harbour Bridge is a photogenic addition to the city's lively harbour scene, visitors can also take a scenic stroll along its pedestrian walkway. The southern entrance is via Cumberland Street in The Rocks. From here, you can walk the length of the Bridge to Milsons Point on the north side. An interesting diversion is to visit the Pylon Lookout, on the southeast side. The Pylon contains a fascinating pictorial history of the Harbour Bridge's construction, and a 200-step climb affords remarkable views. From here you can see the sweep of the harbour to west and east, and much of the city's layout (see pages 26–7).
Tel: 218 6325 for further information.

On the Water

Like moths round a flame, Sydneysiders cannot and will not be kept away from the city's waterways. And why should they? In summer the harbour becomes an evening and weekend magnet for Sydney's overheated and overstressed workers. The water is alive with bobbing craft of all shapes and sizes – from small canoes and sailboards to floating gin palaces and the largest and raciest of million-dollar maxi-yachts, with their smartly uniformed crews. Brightly coloured yellow and green ferries criss-cross the water, and the occasional tanker or container ship makes its careful way into port through this cheerful flotilla.

Special events are an even more remarkable sight. The start of the annual Sydney to Hobart

*Beach and boat life
Manly Bea*

*Billowing sails grace
the Opera House façade*

*Lifeguards in
action at Bondi*

yacht race on 26 December sees the harbour awash with masts, hulls and sails, while on the 1988 Bicentennial Australia Day it was claimed that you could walk from craft to craft across the entire width of the harbour!

Whatever the occasion, or the excuse, Sydney's waterways are a colourful and magic venue. On a sunny day, locals and tourists alike take to the water in their droves – perhaps to eat prawn and mayonnaise sandwiches and down a bottle or two of champagne; to do some serious sailing; or just to sit on a ferry and take in the wonderful vistas of sunshine on sparkling water, hillsides covered with red-tiled roofs, and bushland that has changed little since the arrival of the First Fleet. Life on the water is what this great harbour city is all about.

It's not necessary to opt for high-speed boats

Safe haven – boats at rest

Sydney Opera House and Circular Quay

Sydney may lack a true city centre, but the Opera House and Circular Quay area, framed by the waters of Sydney Harbour, is the undoubted heart of this maritime city. From the Opera House there are fine harbour and bridge views, and Circular Quay is the hub of the city's most enjoyable form of transport – the wonderful harbour ferries, which every visitor should take advantage of.

The Opera House and its nearby attractions can all be reached by taking a train or bus to Circular Quay. The area is also on the Sydney Explorer Bus route.

BENNELONG POINT

The site of the Sydney Opera House was once a small island, separated from the mainland by a shallow channel. In its time the Point has served as the site of Fort Macquarie (1819) and later as a tram depot, demolished to make way for the Opera House. It is named after Bennelong, Governor Arthur Phillip's favourite Aborigine, who was taken to England with Phillip in 1792 and presented to King George III.

Apart from the attraction of viewing the Opera House at close range, Bennelong Point provides an excellent view of the harbour, bridge and the Botanic Gardens. On the north side of the Opera House there is a pleasant outdoor restaurant, where free concerts are held on Sunday afternoons. There is also a Sunday market.

SYDNEY OPERA HOUSE

Construction of Sydney's most famous building began in 1959, but the project was fraught with technical problems and the Opera House was not completed

Love it or loathe it, it cannot be ignored

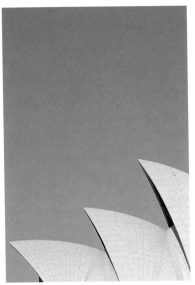

Seem familiar? Detail of the roof

THE REMARKABLE SYDNEY OPERA HOUSE

' ... for there suddenly like an aery fantasy the Sydney Opera House, most peculiar of architectural masterpieces, spreads its white wings in the sunshine, light as some unsuspected water-bird ... '
Jan Morris: *Among the Cities*

Love it or loathe it, the Sydney Opera House is one of the world's most instantly recognisable buildings. Its modernistic white, sail-like roofs and the sheer audacity of its design are all the more remarkable when one considers that Danish architect Joern Utzon's plans were submitted 35 years ago. In 1957 Utzon won an international competition to design an opera house – beating over 200 entries from 32 countries – and Sydney has been left with a lasting mark of his imagination and brilliance.

The Opera House was a technical and administrative nightmare and took 14 years to complete, utilising the skills of over 1,200 people. The original design proved too difficult to execute and had to be modified, and Utzon resigned from the project in 1966, after various disputes with the NSW government.

The roofs of this modern wonder of the world contain more than a million Swedish ceramic tiles, and the vast stone base and terraces are modelled on the Mayan and Aztec temples of Mexico. Despite the construction difficulties, and the grossly inflated cost, the result is a fabulous building that has become an enduring symbol of Sydney and its waterside location.

until 1973, when it was opened, with much fanfare, by Queen Elizabeth II.

The building contains five performance halls and is the home of the Australian national opera and ballet companies. The opera theatre seats 1,500, while the concert hall holds an audience of 2,600. In addition to opera and ballet, the Opera House hosts symphony concerts, theatrical productions and performances of modern music. The complex also includes four restaurants, several bars, shops and an exhibition hall.

Informative guided tours of the interior are conducted daily from 9am to 4pm, and on Sundays visitors can also tour the backstage areas. To really appreciate the interior, however, try to attend a performance during your stay! *Tel: 250 7250. Admission fee for tours of the interior.*

Circular Quay

*Y*es, it's square, but in its time Circular Quay has also been V-shaped and rounded. In the early 1800s, convict labour was used to reclaim the tidal mudflats here and build a horseshoe-shaped retaining wall. Sydney Cove later became the city's major port and wharves were built out into the harbour. The squaring-off process came early this century to create the quay's present shape.

Circular Quay is now the centre of Sydney's busy harbour ferry transport system. The wharves buzz with activity as ferries arrive and depart to destinations north, west and east of the Harbour Bridge. The fast Manly-bound Jetcats also leave from here.

Above the quay there is an unattractive 1960s railway station; this is part of Sydney's small underground City Circle Line, which connects with Town Hall and Central Stations; and the Cahill

Expressway, which leads on to the Harbour Bridge from the eastern suburbs.

Renovations during the 1980s have created a delightful area behind the ferry wharves. Here the visitor can enjoy lunch, coffee, or a snack at outdoor tables with a fine view of the Harbour Bridge and the passing maritime parade as a backdrop. Buskers, jugglers and mime artists often perform here, adding to the constant holiday atmosphere. From this area there is a covered walkway along Circular Quay East, which leads to the Opera House: there are several more outdoor cafés located along this pathway.

CUSTOMS HOUSE
Among the high-rise monsters behind Circular Quay, this 1885 Victorian sandstone building stands proudly as a reminder of how the area once looked. It now contains offices, and is not open to the public. The British flag was first raised by Governor Phillip near here in 1788, and there is an interesting First Fleet memorial sculpture in the square fronting the building.

In front of the Customs House lies Alfred Street: one of the city's major bus interchanges – from which most eastern, southern and western suburbs buses commence their journeys.

The Overseas Passenger Terminal

The Circular Quay at historic Sydney Cove

FIRST FLEET PARK

This small park, which commemorates the people of the 1788 First Fleet, lies in front of the Museum of Contemporary Art and provides a pleasant outlook on the Opera House and water. Several cruise boats also depart from this area.

MUSEUM OF CONTEMPORARY ART

This fine new gallery is located on Circular Quay West (see page 55). The 1930s-designed building is constructed of golden sandstone and is a fine example of the art deco style.

OVERSEAS PASSENGER TERMINAL

Rebuilt in 1987 on the western side of Sydney Cove, the terminal is the mooring point for visiting passenger liners such as the *QE2*. It is a hive of activity when ships are in port, but at other times the building is frequented by diners visiting Doyles and Bilsons, its two excellent waterfront restaurants. Visitors can enjoy a good harbour and Opera House view from the upper deck, which is reached by escalator from Circular Quay West.

SYDNEY COVE

In January 1788, after an eight-month sea journey, a bedraggled and weary bunch of thieves, prostitutes, pickpockets, forgers – and unwilling marines – stepped on to the shores of Sydney Cove. Here, in a strange land far from home, the British flag was raised, tents were pitched, and the isolated colony made its shaky start.

Sydney's life began around this cove, which has continued to play an important role in the city's history. Although the port has long moved west of the Harbour Bridge, Sydney Cove today is important for ferry travel, and is one of the inner city's most important attractions.

Sydney Suburbs

Sydney contains many fascinating suburbs within easy reach of the city centre. The history of the Botany Bay and Parramatta areas goes back to the country's earliest days, while Balmain in the inner west, and the eastern regions of Paddington and Kings Cross, are colourful places to shop and stroll.

BALMAIN

Balmain, named after the First Fleet's Assistant Surgeon, is located on a peninsula which juts out into the harbour, west of the Bridge and opposite The Rocks and Dawes Point. From the 1830s onwards, patches of this land, which had been granted to William Balmain, were sold and the first residences sprang up.

Balmain's somewhat isolated location is perhaps one of the reasons why its history is so well-preserved. Many historic houses remain – from iron lacework-adorned terraces to small stone and weatherboard cottages – that give Balmain a picturesque village atmosphere.

Balmain can be reached by ferry from Circular Quay, or by buses 433 and 434 from The Rocks and George Street.

Darling Street

The suburb's major thoroughfare is named after Sir Ralph Darling, Governor of New South Wales from 1825 to 1831. This is the hub of Balmain and contains many intriguing shops, old hotels and a wide variety of restaurants. A recommended tour is to catch the ferry from Circular Quay to the Darling Street wharf.

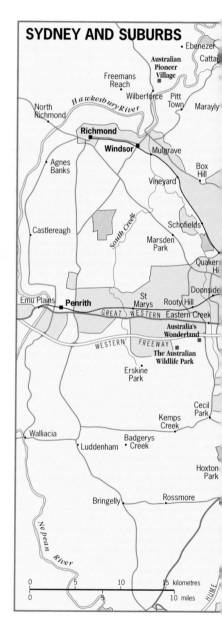

SYDNEY AND SUBURBS

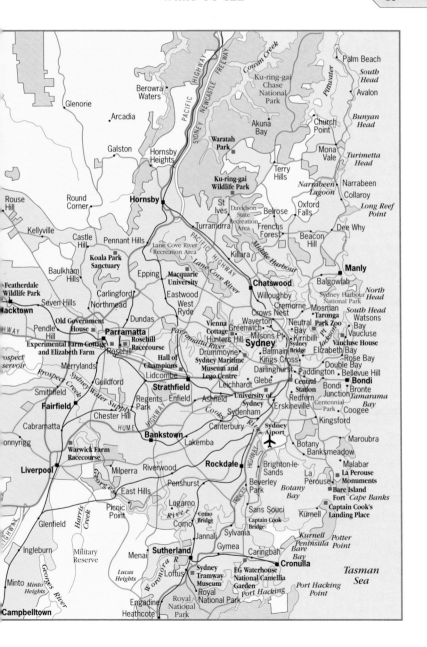

Botany Bay and the South

*W*hen Captain James Cook and the *Endeavour* sailed into this large inlet to the south of Sydney in 1770, Botany Bay was, as it is today, windswept and rather bleak. Cook originally named the area Stingray Bay, but later changed it to Botany Bay after a vast quantity of plants had been collected here by Joseph Banks and his Swedish companion, Dr Solander. The name of Botany Bay later came to be a general term for Port Jackson, Sydney, and even the continent itself.

When the First Fleet departed from Portsmouth in 1787, they were 'bound for Botany Bay', but on arrival found it to be such an inhospitable location for the colony's foundation that they headed further north and discovered the more suitable site of Port Jackson.

BOTANY BAY AND THE GEORGE'S RIVER

Botany Bay has changed a great deal since the 1770s. Since then, a port, oil refineries, red-roofed houses, planes taking off from the nearby airport and huge tankers have disturbed the quiet scene that Cook stumbled upon. It's not the loveliest of Sydney's regions, though the area has a certain, wild appeal. The George's River, however, which flows into the bay from the west, is flanked by some very attractive suburbs.
To reach the north side of Botany Bay, take bus 394 from Circular Quay to the La Perouse terminus.

KURNELL PENINSULA

Kurnell, at the southern side of the bay, is now the province of heavy industry and oil refineries, but the peninsula also contains several historic monuments and a nature reserve with walking trails. The area also offers some good views of Botany Bay.

Captain Cook's Landing Place Historic Site

Cook and his party first landed on Australian soil at Kurnell on 29 April 1770. The site is marked by an obelisk and the area also includes memorials to Joseph Banks and Daniel Solander, and a visitor centre and museum.
Cape Solander Drive, Kurnell Peninsula. Open: weekdays 10.30am–4.30pm, weekends and public holidays to 7pm. Train to Cronulla, then bus 67.

LA PEROUSE

This suburb at the northern side of the bay is named after the Comte de la Perouse, a French explorer who arrived in Botany Bay just six days after the First Fleet in 1788. The party was later lost at sea. There is a monument overlooking the water which marks the arrival of the French.

Near by is the 1882 Old Cable Station, which was built to house operators working on the telegraph line to New Zealand. The Macquarie Watchtower dates from the 1820s and was erected for surveillance of the frequent Botany Bay smuggling activities. Offshore lies Bare Island, which is now linked to the mainland by a bridge. In the 1880s a fort and military barracks were built here as defences against possible French and Russian attacks.

Bare Island Fort – open: daily 9am–5pm. Admission fee. Bus 394 from Circular Quay.

PORT HACKING

This attractive waterway is named after Henry Hacking – Port Jackson's first pilot, and marks the southern limits of the Sydney metropolitan area. To the south lies the undeveloped region of the Royal National Park (see pages 106–7).

THE SOUTHERN SUBURBS

In general, the southern suburbs hold little interest for the visitor. Apart from the Botany Bay area, however, the excellent surf beaches of Cronulla and Maroubra are worth visiting. Their distance from the city also makes them less crowded than beaches to the north.

Maroubra: bus 396 from Circular Quay.

Cronulla: train from Central or Town Hall stations.

SYDNEY (KINGSFORD SMITH) AIRPORT

Sydney's international airport, and the main gateway to Australia, is located just to the north of Botany Bay – the main runway, in fact, juts a considerable distance out into the water. It is named after Sir Charles Kingsford Smith, whose pioneering flights during the 1920s made him internationally famous. The airport is currently undergoing considerable upgrading, including the addition of a third runway, to cope with the recent enormous increase in visitors to Australia.

Open: daily. Airport Express buses from Circular Quay and George Street, or from Kings Cross.

Appropriately named Bare Island

Kings Cross Area

*T*he inner east suburbs of Kings Cross, Potts Point, Elizabeth Bay and Woolloomooloo comprise one of Sydney's most interesting and historic regions. Many visitors will, in fact, find that their hotels are located in this area and the short distance from the city centre makes the district easily accessible. In addition to the transport directions given below, Kings Cross, Elizabeth Bay and Potts Point are on the Sydney Explorer Bus route. Nearby Darlinghurst is also worth a visit, especially for the area's many coffee shops and cheap eating places.

ELIZABETH BAY

Still one of the inner city's most gracious suburbs, Elizabeth Bay grew up around the mansion which bears its name. It is now an area of both old and new apartment blocks and attractive leafy streets and the suburb has its own millionaire's row – Billyard Avenue, which is near Elizabeth Bay House.

Beare Park

Elizabeth Bay's small park and adjoining wharf are right on the harbour. This is a pleasant place for a picnic, or just to sit and look out over the water.
Off Ithaca Road, Elizabeth Bay.

Elizabeth Bay House

This is Sydney's most gracious mansion (see page 56). McElhone Reserve, just in front of the house, provides lovely views down the harbour.

Rushcutters Bay Park

This large park, which has a cricket oval and tennis courts, is adjacent to Elizabeth Bay and affords excellent views of the harbour and Cruising Yacht Club of Australia Marina. It is from here that the famous Sydney to Hobart yacht race commences each Boxing Day.
Via Holdsworth Street, off Elizabeth Bay Road. Train to Kings Cross, or bus 311 from either Circular Quay or Railway Square.

KINGS CROSS

Kings Cross was long considered the 'bohemian' quarter of Sydney, but the Vietnam war years saw the area transformed into a series of bars, clubs and strip joints for military R & R purposes. The bars and clubs are still there, but the area is steadily declining into a province of prostitutes and drug-users. Despite this, it's still a lively, tree-lined suburb with many outdoor cafés – Macleay Street in particular is very

Elegantly restored Elizabeth Bay House

Rushcutters Bay near Kings Cross

pleasant. Numerous hotels, guesthouses and backpackers' lodges are located around Kings Cross, and if you're after restaurants and late nightlife, the 'Cross' is the place to go.
Train from Town Hall or Martin Place.

POTTS POINT

Adjacent to Kings Cross, but a more salubrious suburb, Potts Point is now crammed with backpackers' hostels and budget guesthouses. A stroll from Kings Cross Station down Victoria Street reveals many fine examples of colonial Victorian architecture, and the views of Woolloomooloo Bay and the city from the park at the end of the street are excellent.
Train to Kings Cross from Town Hall or Martin Place.

WOOLLOOMOOLOO

Apart from being the Sydney suburb with the most mis-spelt name (yes, it

does have eight o's!), Woolloomooloo is another historic inner-city enclave. The unusual name is obviously Aboriginal and was first adopted by John Palmer in 1793 for his estate in this area. The suburb is full of sandstone cottages and brick terraced houses which have been colourfully renovated by the Housing Commission. The best way to see Woolloomooloo is to walk down Victoria Street from Kings Cross Station and then descend Butler's Stairs. From here you can wander the streets, and end up at Woolloomooloo Bay, where there are several pleasant pubs. Return to Potts Point via the McElhone Stairs, which lead back to Victoria Street.

Alternatively, the Domain, the Art Gallery of New South Wales, and the Botanic Gardens are to be found just beyond the bay.
Train to Kings Cross.

Café Life

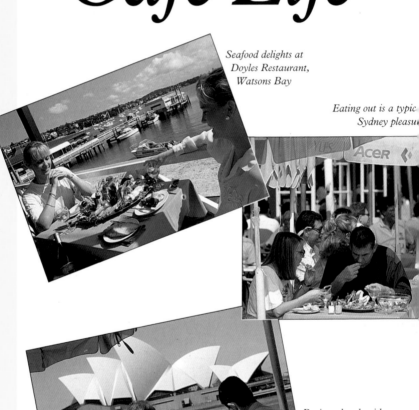

Seafood delights at Doyles Restaurant, Watsons Bay

Eating out is a typic Sydney pleasu

Business lunch with spectacular view

Heading for the beach may be the number one pastime for most Sydneysiders, but for many, hanging out in cafés comes a close second! The post-World War II influx of Italians, in particular, has brought an entire sub-culture to the city and words like cappuccino, espresso, caffè latte, focaccia and Chinotto have become well-entrenched in the collective vocabulary.

Italian-style coffee shops abound – especially around Kings Cross, Darlinghurst and Double Bay, and in the 'little-Italy' suburbs such as Leichhardt in the inner west. Many cafés provide outdoor tables, a perfect way to soak up the sun and watch the world go by. In the Darlinghurst area, such cafés are the province of the bohemian and trendy, especially in the mornings. Even the busiest stockbroker or mobile phone-clutching executive seems to be able to find time for a pre-work sidewalk coffee, croissant and chat. Sydney also specialises in the café with a view. Found particularly at Bondi Beach, Circular Quay and The Rocks, these establishments draw customers like magnets, especially for long lazy weekend breakfasts with a water view.

Outdoor eating is understandably popular in a city with such fine weather. Locals enjoy the many opportunities to dine outdoors at locations like Circular Quay, Kings Cross and The Rocks, or in one of the city's many pub beer gardens – try the Watsons Bay Hotel for fish and chips, beer and wonderful harbour views. There's nothing quite like it on a sunny day.

The more traditionally minded head for tea and cakes at one of the city's fine tea-shops. The best have historic locations – Vaucluse House, the National Trust Centre on Observatory Hill and various spots in Paddington are popular venues for those with English tastes. Whatever the preference, café life has become an integral and welcome part of the Sydney scene.

A pleasant Bayswater brasserie

Paddington and Woollahra

*T*hese inner east suburbs comprise one of the city's most historic, cosmopolitan and attractive districts.

Strolling along Oxford Street, it is difficult to imagine that the present-day charming suburb of Paddington was originally a sandy, swamp-ridden heathland of little interest to the new settlers. In 1811, however, Governor Macquarie had a road constructed through the area *en route* to Watsons Bay, and in 1841 the building of Victoria Barracks led to Paddington's increasing importance. The second half of the 19th century saw rows of terraced workers' houses being built on the suburb's steep hillsides, and it is these streets that give modern-day Paddington its charm. The entire district has been defined as a conservation area by the National Trust so its charms can be preserved.

Today, Paddington is the province of the alternative and the trendy – the original simple terraces have been restored and revamped and now reach high prices on the housing market. The area, centred around Oxford Street, is packed with interesting shops and cafés, and on Saturdays another enjoyable experience is to visit the famous markets (see Shopping). For a fascinating walk around the area see pages 28–9.

The best way to reach Paddington is by bus no 380, which travels from Circular Quay and through the city to Oxford Street.

Hunting for bargains in Paddington Market

AUSTRALIAN CENTRE FOR PHOTOGRAPHY

This interesting gallery features changing photographic exhibitions and also contains a good bookshop.

257 Oxford Street, Paddington. Tel: 331 6253. Open: Wednesday to Saturday 11am–5pm.

CENTENNIAL PARK

Sydney is fortunate to have such a vast expanse of greenery and parkland so close to its centre. The area was originally known as Sydney Common and was used for grazing, but the park had been established by 1888 and was named in honour of Australia's centenary. In January 1901 the Federation ceremony, which formally established the Australian Commonwealth, took place here. Centennial Park has ponds, sports fields, cycling and horse riding tracks, an excellent café and many hectares of grassland. Open-air concerts are regularly held here.

Main entrance: at the corner of Oxford Street and Lang Road, Paddington. Open: daily during daylight hours.

JUNIPER HALL

Built by Robert Cooper from the profits of his gin distillery in 1824, Juniper Hall is a simple colonial-style house that was later used as a child welfare institution. The building is the oldest existing dwelling east of Sydney city and now belongs to the National Trust. It contains an excellent NT gift shop and tea-rooms, as well as the Museum of Australian Childhood (see page 154).
248 Oxford Street, Paddington.
Tel: 332 1988. Open: Tuesday to Sunday 10am–4pm. Admission fee to museum.

VICTORIA BARRACKS

This historic complex was begun in 1841 as a replacement for the colony's original military barracks on Observatory Hill. The impressive 225m-long sandstone building is an excellent example of the Regency architectural style and is still occupied by the army. Tours take in the barracks, a military museum and the pleasant grounds.
Oxford Street, Paddington. Tel: 339 3543. Open: Tuesdays at 10am for tours; first Sunday of each month 1.30pm–4.30pm.

Museum of Australian Childhood

WOOLLAHRA: QUEEN STREET

Running off the top end of Paddington's Oxford Street, tree-lined Queen Street is one of the inner city's most exclusive shopping precincts. Here you will find smart clothing and gift shops, delicatessens and restaurants. The thoroughfare also contains a host of Sydney's best antique shops, as well as establishments specialising in rare books and prints. The Woollahra Hotel, at the junction with Moncur Street, has good food and a nice beer garden.

The insignia of the Barracks Museum

Village Life

Sydney seems to specialise in small, compact mini-suburbs which are very unlike the vast, densely populated districts of a city such as London or New York. Within many of these inner-city areas a true village feeling has developed, creating unique atmospheres which visitors will also enjoy.

Balmain's peninsular setting has led to the existence of a tight-knit village community. Originally a suburb for dockside workers, much gentrification has taken place, but the imported yuppie element still rubs shoulders with the working-class man in many of the suburb's abundant and popular pubs.

A very different kind of village life is to be found in Double Bay. In this enclave of the rich and glamorous you are more likely to see well-heeled café-goers gliding out of their Porsches and Jaguars. Double Bay, along with the nearby suburb of Bellevue Hill, is the home of many wealthy Europeans and Jews who create a truly cosmopolitan atmosphere and sense of street life.

Glebe's proximity to Sydney University has made it the home of many of the city's students. Here you will see the youthful 'all-in-black brigade', and experience an interesting area that is full of bookshops, cafés and unusual second-hand clothing shops.

Over in the eastern suburbs, Paddington has perhaps the best 'village' atmosphere of anywhere in Sydney. The community here is made up of all sorts of people from gays to glitterati, or from the arty set to hippies. Cafés abound, as do interesting and offbeat shops. The best time to be here is on a Saturday, when Paddington really comes alive through its colourful bazaar, held in the grounds of a local church.

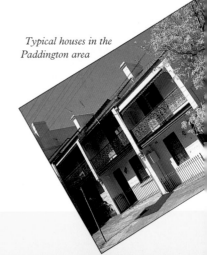

Typical houses in the Paddington area

Paddington's market - the
area comes alive

Shopping for fresh food
in Darling Street, Balmain

The London Hotel,
Balmain

Kirribilli Street -
attractive village
community

Parramatta and the Western Suburbs

*T*oday, suburban Parramatta is a city in its own right and the heartland of Sydney's vast metropolitan area, but almost 200 years ago the settlement was an outpost of Sydney Town – 24km away by rough track, or by boat up the Parramatta River.

The nation's second oldest settlement was founded in November 1788, just a few months after the arrival of the First Fleet. Initial delight at the discovery of Port Jackson's fine harbour turned to disappointment with the realisation that the soil was poor and rocky. The fate of the colony depended on fertile farming land, and this was found west of Sydney Cove, at the head of the river which flowed into Port Jackson.

The settlers cleared land here in 1788 and began farming. Within a short time, Rose Hill, as it was then known, had developed into not only the agricultural centre of the colony, but also the social and cultural hub. The first rough buildings were erected in July 1789 and a township was formed in the following year.

Parramatta is reached by a 30-minute train journey from Town Hall or Central stations.

Elizabeth Farm

The building of this cottage began in 1793 and it contains remnants of Australia's oldest European building. It was once the home of agricultural pioneers John and Elizabeth Macarthur, who introduced merino sheep into the colony. The well-preserved house is a fine example of early colonial architecture and features wide, shady verandahs to combat the fierce summer sun. The farm is furnished in period style and set in a beautiful 1830s garden.
70 Alice Street, Parramatta. Tel: 635 9488. Open: Tuesday to Sunday 10am–4.30pm. Admission fee includes a guided tour.

Experiment Farm Cottage

This cottage is set on a very historic piece of land. In 1792 Governor Phillip made the colony's first land grant to ex-convict James Ruse, as an experiment in agricultural self-sufficiency. Ruse proved that this was indeed possible and later

Beautifully furnished Experiment Farm

sold the fertile land to Colonial Surgeon John Harris, who built the present cottage in 1835. The building has been well restored and is furnished in the period style of the early 1800s.

9 Ruse Street, Parramatta. Tel: 635 5655. Open: Tuesday to Thursday, and Sunday 10am–5pm. Admission fee.

Old Government House

Dating from 1799, this is the nation's oldest public building. Located in Parramatta's attractive park, it was built for Governor Phillip but was greatly extended between 1815 and 1816 by a later occupant, Governor Macquarie. In the early years this vice-regal residence was the home of the colony's, albeit limited, high society, far removed from the convict sweat and toil at Sydney Cove. Government House is now under the care of the National Trust and is furnished with a collection of pre-1850 pieces. Also in Parramatta Park are the remains of Australia's first observatory (1822) and the 1823 Governor's Bath House.

Parramatta Park. Tel: 635 8149. Open: Tuesday to Thursday, and Sunday 10am–4pm. Admission fee.

Parramatta Tourist Information Centre

Parramatta contains many other interesting buildings, such as Hambledon Cottage, built in 1824; the Georgian Harrisford House which dates from the 1820s; Brislington, an 1821 residence and now a museum of local medical history and St John's Church and cemetery (1850s). Details of these and other Parramatta sites are available from the tourist centre which also offers a leaflet describing a self-guided walking tour of the city.

Government House in Parramatta's park

Prince Alfred Park, Market Street. Tel: 630 3703. Open: daily 9am–5pm.

THE WESTERN SUBURBS

Most of the western suburbs' urban sprawl contains little to interest the visitor, but there are a couple of attractions *en route* to Parramatta.

Drummoyne and Birkenhead Point

The attractive harbourside suburb of Drummoyne includes Birkenhead Point, a shopping and market centre which can be reached by a ferry trip. This is also the location for the Sydney Maritime Museum. The museum contains various displays, the highlight of which is a number of historic ships.

Off Victoria Road, Drummoyne. Tel: 818 5388. Open: Tuesday to Sunday 10am–5pm, Monday 1.30pm–5pm. Ferry from Circular Quay, or bus 500 from Town Hall.

State Sports Centre

This well-equipped sports centre features the NSW Hall of Champions, a museum dedicated to the state's sporting heroes from 1876 to the present day.

Australia Avenue, Homebush. Tel: 746 2855. Open: daily 8.30am–5pm. Train to North Strathfield.

Unknown Sydney

*E*very city has its nooks and crannies which are off the beaten tourist track, and Sydney is no exception. The visitor with plenty of time to spare will enjoy these lesser-known attractions that range from museums to harbourside suburbs.

Other little-known corners of Sydney are included in **Getting Away From It All** – see pages 130–141.

CREMORNE POINT

This northern harbourside suburb is one of the city's most pleasant, and is just a short ride from Circular Quay. From the Cremorne wharf you can walk through a reserve either to the right to Mosman Bay, or around the Point to Shell Cove. The latter area includes the small, saltwater MacCallum Pool, which is great for a refreshing swim with harbour views. The entire reserve has a magnificent harbour outlook, yet is uncrowded (except at weekends) and tourist-free.
Ferry from Circular Quay to Cremorne Point.

HUNTERS HILL

Hunters Hill is one of the city's most scenic and expensive harbour suburbs, reached by a pleasant ferry ride from Circular Quay. The suburb is also home to Vienna Cottage, a house dating from 1871 (see page 57).
Ferry to Valentia Street Wharf from Circular Quay.

NORTH SYDNEY, MILSON'S POINT, KIRRIBILLI AND MCMAHON'S POINT

To the north of the Harbour Bridge, this area is one that few visitors get a chance to explore. North Sydney is best described as a smaller version of the CBD (Central Business District): the area is full of office blocks and shops and is the centre for Sydney's advertising, computer and creative industries. Near by, the suburbs of Milson's Point,

A wharf sign in leafy Hunter's Hill

Kirribilli - pleasant Sydney suburb

McMahon's Point and Kirribilli offer some surprises, though. Milson's Point contains the delightful North Sydney Olympic Swimming Pool, and from here there is a nice walk around Lavender Bay to McMahon's Point. This suburb is full of delightful 19th-century houses, and a walk down Blues Point Road to the ferry wharf and park is most enjoyable. Kirribilli contains Admiralty House and Kirribilli House, the Sydney residences of the Governor General and Prime Minister respectively (see pages 26–7).
Train to Milson's Point or North Sydney; ferry to McMahon's Point or Kirribilli.

ROSE BAY
Rose Bay is one of the city's many harbourside suburbs, but it is blessed with a particularly long water frontage and great harbour views. It was named in the early days of the colony by Governor Phillip in honour of George Rose, Secretary to the Treasury. Rose Bay is the city's most popular sailboarding

venue and the area also has tennis courts, a golf course and various parks. It's a great spot for picnics and general harbour-watching. At weekends, a ferry service from Circular Quay calls in at Rose Bay on its way to Taronga Zoo and Watsons Bay – the trip makes a great day out on the Harbour.
Bus 324/325 (or ferry at weekends) from Circular Quay.

UNIVERSITY OF SYDNEY
Australia's oldest university was founded in 1850 and the site includes grand buildings and quadrangles in the Oxford and Cambridge tradition which date from this era. The Great Hall is another reminder of the university's English roots. The Macleay Museum here contains a fine natural history and Aboriginal cultural collection.
Parramatta Road, Broadway. Tel: 692 2274. Open: Tuesday to Friday 8.30am– 4.30pm. Admission free. Buses 435–440 from George Street.

Fragrantly named Lavender Bay

The Blue Mountains

*A*lthough not really mountains, this heavily forested section of the Great Dividing Range proved to be an impenetrable and frustrating barrier to the early settlers. It was not until 1813 that the explorers Blaxland, Wentworth and Lawson found a route through this beautiful area of sandstone plateaux, deep gorges and rivers to the farming lands of the west.

Today, the Blue Mountains are one of Sydney's favourite recreation areas. Despite their proximity to the city – a mere 100km away – and increasing urban development, they remain very much a wilderness area, little changed since the days of the first European arrivals. There are three rugged national parks in the region – the Blue Mountains, Wollemi and Kanangra Boyd – and the bushwalking, climbing, horse riding and cycling opportunities here are almost endless.

BELL'S LINE OF ROAD

Most visitors take the Great Western Highway to the Mountains, but this alternative, northern route is much more scenic. The winding road passes through the small apple-growing towns of Bilpin and Kurrajong and there are also some notable gardens in the region.

BLACKHEATH

From just outside this small town there

The dramatic landscape of Kanangra

are wonderful views into the Grose Valley, on the northern side of the Great Western Highway. Head for Evans Lookout and Govetts Leap for the best panoramas. Blackheath is also famous for its lovely rhododendron gardens.

Queuing for a view of the Three Sisters

JENOLAN CAVES

If you have time, a detour from Mount Victoria to Australia's most famous cave system is worthwhile. The interesting caves contain many stalactites and stalagmites and are part of a 2,500-hectare wildlife reserve. The area is on the borders of yet another challenging region of these mountains:

the Kanangra Boyd National Park.
Open: daily 9am–5.30pm. Admission fee.

KATOOMBA

The major town of the Blue Mountains area also contains the most important sights. Katoomba developed originally as an 1841 coal-mining settlement, but has long been a popular tourist resort and contains many hotels and guesthouses. The town has an interesting main street – visit the 1930s art deco Paragon Café – and a number of galleries, antique shops and museums.

Echo Point and the Three Sisters

There are wonderful views from this viewpoint over the thickly forested Jamison Valley, including a bird's-eye view of the Three Sisters. This unusual geological formation features in Aboriginal legends and is one of the area's highlights. You can also view the marvellous scenery from the Scenic Skyway, or take a ride on the Scenic Railway down into the Jamison Valley.

LEURA

Katoomba's small neighbour is the region's most attractive town, containing many lovely old houses and antique shops: the main street is National Trust listed. Also at Leura is Leuralla, a 1914 stately home which contains a fine collection of 19th-century Australian art. Katoomba and Leura are linked by a scenic clifftop drive, which is a must.
Open: Friday to Sunday 10am–5pm.

LOWER BLUE MOUNTAINS

There are several attractions in this lower section of the mountains. At Glenbrook there is a useful tourist centre beside the main road, and a native plant reserve. Further along the Great Western

Katoomba, the major town in the area

Highway, Faulconbridge features the interesting Norman Lindsay Gallery and Museum, which is well signposted from the highway. Lindsay was one of Australia's most accomplished writers, artists and sculptors. Just before Leura, Wentworth Falls contains a reserve which overlooks the waterfalls, and is also the site of Yester Grange – a restored Victorian country house which is open to the public.
Norman Lindsay Gallery and Museum, Faulconbridge. Open: Friday to Sunday 11am–5pm. Yester Grange, Wentworth Falls. Open: Friday to Sunday 10am–5pm.

MOUNT VICTORIA

Mount Victoria's high elevation of 1,111m makes it a chilly place to be in winter, but the town contains several historic buildings, including the old Victoria and Albert Hotel, and the entire settlement is classified as an Urban Conservation Area. At nearby Mount York there are monuments which are dedicated to the early Blue Mountains explorers, and the lookout here offers more breathtaking views.

The Central Coast

*T*he Central Coast region begins just north of Sydney, across the waters of Broken Bay, and stretches up the coast to include lakes, inlets, small towns and the large industrial city of Newcastle. The region's beautiful waterways and coast, two national parks, and its proximity to the state's largest cities, have made it a popular holiday destination and, increasingly, a commuter belt for both Sydney and Newcastle.

BEACHES

The Central Coast area has some wonderful beaches – ranging from the surfing havens on the coast around Terrigal and Newcastle, to the quiet bays and inlets of the lakes and waterways around Gosford and The Entrance.

BOUDDI NATIONAL PARK

To the southeast of Gosford, 1150-hectare Bouddi National Park takes in much of the dramatic and deeply indented coast of Maitland Bay, and also includes inland areas of rainforest, heathland and fern groves. There are golden sands and good swimming at Putty, Tallow and Little Beaches; campsites are also located here. Entry into the park is via Gosford and the Pacific Highway, or Woy Woy and the Rip Bridge.

BRISBANE WATER NATIONAL PARK

Bounded by the Hawkesbury River and Broken Bay to the south, and Gosford and Brisbane Water to the east, this is one of the state's most attractive marine parks. Much of the region is sandstone, which supports the heath and woodland cover that is so typical of the Sydney region, with pockets of rainforest interspersed among the less exotic vegetation. The park also contains some lovely unspoiled beaches, and Aboriginal rock carvings and has a large and varied bird population. Access is from the Pacific Highway to the west of Gosford, or from the small town of Woy Woy. *Further information on both of these national parks is available from the Gosford office of the National Parks and Wildlife Service. Tel: (043) 24 4911.*

GOSFORD

Located 85km north of Sydney, and reached by a fast train service, the pleasant town of Gosford has become a part of the city's commuter belt. The town is at the head of Brisbane Water and is surrounded by an agricultural belt, specialising in vegetable, fruit and timber growing. Its proximity to Sydney and nearby beaches have also made it a popular holiday retreat.

NEWCASTLE

New South Wales's second largest city, with a population of around 423,000, is 170km north of Sydney. Although best known as a mining and industrial centre, Newcastle has an attractive location at the mouth of the Hunter River and the area contains eight excellent beaches, which are very popular with surfers. Coal was discovered here as early as 1791, and in the early 1800s the mines of this outpost were used as a place of hard labour for particularly difficult convicts.

From 1850 onwards, Newcastle developed into a major port and a coal-mining region, with steelworks and ship-building yards being added during the 1920s.

In addition to its beaches, Newcastle contains an interesting Maritime and Military Museum, the Regional Art Gallery and some grand Victorian buildings. The city is also an ideal starting point for trips into the Hunter Valley wine region, and for excursions to Myall Lakes National Park and other coastal areas to the north.

Newcastle Region Maritime and Military Museum. Open: Tuesday to Sunday noon–4pm.
Newcastle Regional Art Gallery. Open: Monday to Friday 10am–5pm, weekends 2pm–5pm.

Lake Macquarie

Just 27km south of Newcastle, this large waterway is the largest saltwater lake in Australia. Its shores are well-populated, but the attractive lake offers excellent opportunities for watersports, and is surrounded by parks, picnic areas and a cycleway.

TERRIGAL

This town, between Bouddi National Park and The Entrance, is one of the area's nicest resorts, and not unlike an English seaside town. The beaches are good and Terrigal also offers some excellent hotels and eating places.

TUGGERAH LAKES

South of Newcastle, this region contains three attractive lakes – Tuggerah, Budgewoi and Munmorah – and is served by the tourist resorts of The Entrance and Toukley. On the coast there are some good surfing and swimming opportunities, while the inland lakes are excellent for boating.

Tranquillity on Lake Macquarie

Ku-ring-gai Chase National Park and Pittwater

*A*rguably the metropolitan area's most attractive waterway, Pittwater is bounded by exclusive suburbs such as Newport, Clareville and Palm Beach. These contain the water-view homes of the wealthy, and those whose creative pursuits such as writing and the media permit them to work from home, rather than driving the 40km or so into the city each day. The area is, however, remarkable in that it is so close to Sydney, yet has retained most of its unspoiled natural beauty. Much of this is due to the presence of the Ku-ring-gai Chase National Park on the western side of the waterway which has much to offer the visitor.

The eastern and southern sides of Pittwater are reached via Pittwater and Barrenjoey Roads (to Palm Beach), while access into the national park is by scenic routes from either Mona Vale Road at Terrey Hills, or the Bobbin Head Road turnoff from the Pacific Highway at Pymble. There is a good visitor centre at Bobbin head.

COWAN CREEK

From the national park's Bobbin Head picnic area and Park Information Centre, Cowan Creek and its various branches meander their way northeast to join the Hawkesbury River and Broken Bay. The waterway is best explored by boat, but there are bushwalking tracks which follow the shoreline. You can also visit Bobbin Head by a scenic and relaxing ferry trip from Palm Beach.

KU-RING-GAI CHASE NATIONAL PARK

Dedicated in 1894, 14,712-hectare Ku-ring-gai is Australia's second oldest national park. The terrain here is rugged sandstone bush and woodland, and the park is flanked by the lovely waterways of Pittwater, the Hawkesbury River and Berowra Creek. From these drowned river valleys the Ku-ring-gai plateau rises 250m to create a bushland area that is home to over 170 species of birds, and

one that is popular with picnickers and bushwalkers. The waterways, too, provide almost endless recreational possibilities.

The name of the area is obviously Aboriginal and relates to the tribe that once lived and hunted here: there are many Aboriginal carvings within the park. Information on these fascinating remnants of an ancient culture, bushwalking and all park activities are available from the Kalkari Visitor Centre near Bobbin Head.
Guided walks. Tel: 457 9853. Open: daily 9am–4.30pm daily. Closed: noon–1pm.

PITTWATER

This lovely waterway received one of the colony's earliest names when it was so named by Governor Phillip in 1788 after William Pitt, the British Prime Minister. Although the eastern shores have developed into an exclusive residential area, the unspoiled western side is part

Pittwater is a paradise of natural beauty

of Ku-ring-gai Chase National Park. The area is popular with sailors, windsurfers and canoeists and contains many hidden bays and inlets which are accessible only by boat.

Visitors can explore the waterway by taking a ferry ride from the inland side of Palm Beach.

Palm Beach

The delightful suburb of Palm Beach not only has an oceanfront, it also borders Pittwater. On this calm-water side there is a pleasant beach, with a jetty for ferry services across the water to Bobbin Head, Mackerel Beach and other locations on the shores of Ku-ring-gai.

Barrenjoey Head

On the eastern side of Pittwater, Barrenjoey Head and its lighthouse perch 113m above the water. The unusual name is Aboriginal for a young kangaroo. The Head sprouts up dramatically from the utterly flat beach below and marks the entrance into Broken Bay and the Hawkesbury River from the Pacific Ocean.

UPPER HAWKESBURY RIVER

From its unspectacular beginnings in the Great Dividing Range, the Hawkesbury is transformed by the time it reaches the sea at Broken Bay, to the north of Pittwater. When the river takes its final turn into the ocean here, it has become a magnificent, wide, aquatic playground. The best way to explore this delightful area is again by boat – yachts, power boats and houseboats are all available for hire.

The Bush

The Australian bush is quite unique. Even today, visitors from the northern hemisphere will not find it difficult to imagine the surprise of the First Fleeters on sighting this apparent wilderness of sandstone plateaux and heathland; the home of pale-trunked eucalypts, strange plants and flowers and exotic wildlife.

Despite the increasing urbanisation of the state's coastal areas, large pockets of bushland remain. And in many parts inland, where settlement is sparse and distances between towns are large, little has changed since the 1780s. From the rainforests in the sub-tropical north, to the high alpine terrain of the Snowy Mountains, the New South Wales countryside offers unlimited opportunities for rest and recreation away from the city rush.

Much of this land is contained in the state's many national parks, which encompass everything from coastal cliffs and beaches to dramatic mountain ranges and, in the west and north, wild outback. There are many ways to appreciate these unspoiled regions, but the best is undoubtedly on foot. Bushwalking is very popular, and even quite close to Sydney there are many opportunities for the activity. You can walk the coastal path of the Royal National Park, or enjoy the water views in Ku-ring-gai Chase – just a few kilometres from the city centre.

In such areas there is an astonishing variety of plants. There are some 20,000 species altogether in Australia, more than 80 per cent of which are unique to the continent. Take time to view the state's lovely wildflowers: banksias, boronia, Christmas bells, bottlebrush, acacias, wattle and the magnificent waratah, the floral emblem of NSW. You will also encounter unfamiliar plants and trees such as cabbage tree palms, exotic ferns and casuarina trees. Even the good old gum tree comes in an amazing range of forms: blue gums, scribbly gums, snow gums and river red gums are just some varieties of the ubiquitous and unmistakably Australian eucalypt.

*Coastal Banksia attrac
a variety of birds an
insec*

...ksia Ericifolius burns with
...ur in the Australian

*A White
Gum, one of Australia's
many eucalypts*

*A grim warning
for travellers in the
bush*

*The unusual
Eucalyptus caesia*

Richmond, Windsor and the Upper Hawkesbury

*T*his region on the northwest border of the metropolitan area was first explored by boat, along the Hawkesbury River, by Governor Phillip in 1789. Although the area was initially considered to be too isolated for settlement, the colony was desperately in need of good agricultural land and the soil of this river region proved to be ideal.

The first farming began here in the early 1790s, but flooding soon became a problem and Governor Macquarie established his five 'Macquarie Towns' in 1810, as settlements above the flood plain. These historic towns – Richmond, Windsor, Pitt Town, Wilberforce and Castlereagh – form the core of one of Sydney's most interesting regions.

A visit to Richmond and Windsor can easily be combined with a trip to the Blue Mountains (see pages 96–7). Two days is recommended for such an outing.

CATTAI STATE RECREATION AREA

This 223-hectare reserve is on the banks of the Hawkesbury and offers opportunities for fishing, boating, walking and horse riding. Cattai is located north of Pitt Town; access to the area is off Wiseman's Ferry Road.

St Matthew's Church at Windsor

EBENEZER

The small village of Ebenezer, near Cattai, contains Australia's oldest place of worship. The Presbyterian Church here dates from 1809 and was built by Scottish settlers.

HAWKESBURY RIVER

The upper reaches of the Hawkesbury wind their way from the Great Dividing Range through the region, *en route* to Broken Bay and the ocean to the north of Sydney. In the early days, before a road was built to Windsor and Richmond, the river was the major means of transportation and communication with Sydney. Today it provides wonderful recreation possibilities: fishing, canoeing and rowing are all popular sports in the region.

RICHMOND

Historic Richmond dates from 1810, but its position bordering the Windsor Road has led to it becoming more developed than the other towns of the region. There are, however, many old buildings and churches dating from the mid-1800s. Richmond is also the home of the Hawkesbury Agricultural College, established in 1891.

RAAF Base

First established in 1925, this base near Richmond is Australia's largest airforce establishment, with over 2,500 personnel. A popular air show is held here annually.
Open: only on special occasions. Tel: (045) 70 3111 for details.

WILBERFORCE

The interesting little village of Wilberforce, just north of Windsor, contains the Australiana Pioneer Village, a re-creation of an early 19th-century settlement (see page 155).
Open: Wednesday to Sunday 10am–5pm. Admission fee.

WINDSOR

The first settlers arrived here in 1794 and the town was laid out in 1810. Many charming old buildings remain, such as the 1815 Macquarie Arms Hotel, the Daniel O'Connell Inn

(1840s) and the 1879 Observatory.

Pitt Town

To the northeast of Windsor, this village was one of the original Macquarie towns and has retained several historic buildings. There are residences which date from the 1820s, as well as St James (1857) and the Scots Church (1862).

St Matthew's Church

This lovely Windsor church dates from 1820 and was designed by Francis Greenway, the architect of Hyde Park Barracks and many of Sydney's most historic buildings.
Moses Street. Open: daily.

WISEMAN'S FERRY

Solomon Wiseman was one of the early settlers here, to the north of the Richmond and Windsor area. He established an inn and a ferry service across the Hawkesbury in 1817, which was followed by a convict-built road through the region in 1826. The area is well-known for dairying and vegetable growing and Wiseman's Ferry itself is an attractive little settlement on the river banks.

An ideal place to stop over

The Royal and Heathcote National Parks

*S*ydney is indeed fortunate. Not only is she blessed with sunshine and surrounded by water, but the city is ringed with unspoiled and easily accessible areas of natural beauty. One of the most attractive of these is just to the south of the urban sprawl – in fact, this green belt forms the metropolitan area's southern limit.

ROYAL NATIONAL PARK

Australia's oldest (and the world's second oldest) national park was established way back in 1879. The Royal is less than an hour's drive from Sydney along the Princes Highway, or you can travel by train to Loftus in a similar time. This proximity to the city makes the park less of a wilderness region than many people would like, but it is still a most attractive recreation area. A car is recommended, however, as there is much to explore within the park. If you have limited time and want a flavour of the place, follow Lady Carrington Drive from Audley to Garie Beach.

The national park's terrain is best described as coastal heathland with scattered eucalypt forests, and it contains some of the Sydney region's most beautiful beaches in its 21km stretch of coastline. There is plenty of birdlife here too (over 200 varieties), and you are likely to encounter brightly coloured rosellas, cockatoos and kookaburras.

Audley

Located on the Hacking River, Audley contains the National Park Station and a Visitor Centre, which provide useful information on the park. Rowing boats and canoes are available for hire here, and there are also toilets and food and drink outlets.

A vibrant sky above the national park

A tempting glimpse of Era Beach

Beaches

The beaches of the Royal National Park are close to heaven for anyone interested in watersports, or just ocean scenery. The undoubted gem of the park is Garie Beach: a long stretch of golden sand, clean water and cliffs which is easily reached by car. There is a surf club here and on weekends the beach can become quite crowded. Garie and Era Beaches are the best spots for surfing. Another beach which is accessible by road is Wattamolla, further to the north. There is a lagoon behind the beach and the area has facilities such as a refreshment kiosk and toilets. Some other beaches which are less accessible, and obviously not so crowded, are Burning Palms in the south and Marley and Little Marley in the park's northern section.

Bushwalks

Walking opportunities abound in the Royal. One of the best walks in the entire Sydney region is the 30km coastal track from Bundeena, on the shores of Port Hacking, to Otford, at the southern end of the park. Two days are needed to undertake this, but there are many shorter jaunts. Full details are available from the Visitor Centre at Audley, or any National Parks and Wildlife Service office.

HEATHCOTE NATIONAL PARK

The Royal's smaller neighbour is bordered by the Woronora River to the west and the Princes Highway on its eastern side. This park of over 2,000 hectares is a dry heath and eucalyptus environment, criss-crossed by a number of creeks. There are some good bushwalking possibilities here, and the Heathcote National Park is generally less crowded than the Royal.

SYDNEY TRAMWAY MUSEUM

This is just off the Princes Highway at Loftus, near the entrance to the Royal National Park. The complex contains a large number of old buses and tramcars, which were common in Sydney until 1961, as well as a restored electric tram which operates on a short stretch of track.

Rawson Avenue, Loftus. Tel: 521 7624. Open: Sundays and public holidays 10am–5pm. Admission fee.

The Southern Highlands and the South Coast

*T*he scenery of this region varies from rugged and unmistakably Australian bushland, to scenes that are straight out of village England – expect to see tea and cricket on the green at Bowral, rolling hills, orchards and farmland. First settled in the 1820s, this fertile upland area attracted farmers and other settlers who moved south from Sydney. There is much to interest the visitor: historic houses, picturesque towns and villages, a national park and some attractive coastal scenery. Wollongong, NSW's third largest city (after Sydney and Newcastle), is also within this region.

The Southern Highlands is convenient-ly reached by either of two routes: the inland Hume Highway, or the Princes Highway which passes Wollongong and Kiama.

BERRIMA
The lovely town of Berrima, 123km from Sydney, is Australia's best preserved Georgian settlement. It began life in 1829 and contains buildings such as the Surveyor-General Hotel, which has been catering to Hume Highway travellers since 1834. The Holy Trinity Church dates from the 1840s, while the Court House and Gaol were completed by 1839. The town is also famous for its craft and antique shops and many tea-rooms.
Berrima Court House, Gaol and other historic buildings. Open: daily 10am–4pm.

Life in Berrima moves to a gentler rhythm, and arts and crafts flourish

BOWRAL
More English than England, Bowral is a pretty, tree-lined town which dates from 1862. It contains numerous gardens and fine houses, which were built to accom-modate the many holiday-makers and retirees who began to move into the area late last century. Bowral's main claim to fame is that the town was the birthplace of Sir Donald Bradman, the famous cricketer. The cricket pavilion here contains an interesting Bradman museum.
Sir Donald Bradman Museum. Open: daily 10am–5pm.

BUNDANOON
Perched on a plateau, above Morton National Park, Bundanoon is a popular

holiday town. It is located on the railway line and contains several guesthouses and cafés. From here there are many walks into the rugged wilderness of the national park.

KANGAROO VALLEY

This is not just the name of the beautiful green, pastoral valley which lies at the bottom of the nearby sandstone escarpment, but also of the small and historic village at its heart. There are many old buildings here, and also the interesting Pioneer Settlement Museum complex.
Pioneer Settlement Museum. Open: daily 10am–4pm. Admission fee.

KIAMA

First discovered by explorer George Bass in 1797, the small coastal town of Kiama developed into a fishing port during the 19th century and is now a popular holiday resort. The town's main attraction is its blowhole, through which the sea rushes noisily, but the port and harbour are also of interest, and the town has several fine old buildings.

MORTON NATIONAL PARK

Not unlike the Blue Mountains area in appearance, the Morton National Park contains deep sandstone gorges, rivers and thick eucalyptus forests. This wilderness area is great for adventurous bushwalking and features a wide variety of wildflowers, plants and birdlife.

MOSS VALE

Moss Vale developed primarily as a market centre for the surrounding pastoral districts, and today it is an attractive town which features lovely gardens and many antiques and craft shops.

Woodcraft in Kangaroo Valley

SUTTON FOREST

This hamlet near Moss Vale contains Hillview, a mansion which was once the country residence of State Governors. The house remains, but is not open to the public. The village has many other grand homes dating from the 1880s.

WOLLONGONG

The third largest city in New South Wales lies at the foot of the steep Illawarra Plateau, some 82km south of Sydney, and has a population of around 230,000. Primarily a port and heavy industrial centre, the city also has some fine beaches and the attractive recreation area of Lake Illawarra, to its south. This university city contains other visitor attractions in its excellent Art Gallery and Historical Society Museum.
Wollongong City Art Gallery. Open: Tuesday to Sunday 10am–5pm.
Illawarra Historical Society Museum. Open: Wednesday 10am–4pm, weekends 1.30pm– 4.30pm.

Canberra and the Australian Capital Territory (ACT)

*C*anberra, the national capital, is located just 300km southwest of Sydney. The site for the capital was chosen in 1908, as a result of the constant bickering between the cities of Sydney and Melbourne for that honour. Although Canberra is geographically a part of New South Wales, the Australian Capital Territory (ACT) was formed as a separate territory to suppress any further arguments about which state contained the capital. The city is planned as a series of circular roads and satellite suburbs, and is occupied mostly by students, public servants and government officials. The Prime Minister's official residence, The Lodge, is located in Canberra.

Other than those listed below, Canberra has many other attractions, including the Australian National University, the Australian Institute of Sport, the Royal Military College and Tidbinbilla Space Tracking Station. Detailed information on Canberra and the ACT is available from the Canberra Tourist Bureau *(tel: 008 026 166)*.

CANBERRA
Australian War Memorial

Interestingly, this is one of the nation's most visited attractions. The vast, domed building contains a museum, art gallery, various memorials and a library and is fronted by an attractive courtyard. From here, the grand avenue of Anzac Parade stretches down to Lake Burley Griffin.

Open: daily 9am–4.45pm. Admission fee.

Black Mountain and the Australian National Botanic Gardens

Canberra's attractive Botanic Gardens contain some short, interesting walks: the Aboriginal Trail and rainforest strolls are particularly pleasant. Black Mountain, behind the gardens, is topped by a telecommunications tower and provides excellent views of the city and surrounding area.

Australian National Botanic Gardens. Open: daily 9am–5pm.

Sun-filled interior of Parliament House

Lake Burley Griffin

Named after Canberra's architect, man-made Lake Burley Griffin is the city's centrepiece. The park-fringed lake was created in 1964 and has a 35km foreshore. There is a cycle track and footpath around the lake, which is very popular with sailors, windsurfers and other aquatic sports enthusiasts. Special features of the lake include the Captain Cook Memorial Water Jet and a carillon, which was donated by the British government.

National Gallery of Australia

A visit to the nation's largest art gallery is highly recommended. It contains representation of all phases of Aboriginal and Australian art, as well as works of art from Europe, Asia and the Pacific. The gallery also has pleasant, sculpture-filled gardens and an excellent restaurant and shop.
Open: daily 10am–5pm. Admission fee.

Parliament House

This new, futuristic-style building stands high on Capital Hill, overlooking the lake, and dwarfs the 1927 'Old' Parliament House below. The building was completed as a 1988 Bicentennial project and contains reception halls, meeting rooms and the two main parliamentary chambers: the House of Representatives and the Senate. The building is capped by an 81m flagpole, and there are excellent views of the city from the roof.
Open: daily 9am–5pm.

WITHIN THE ACT
Lanyon Homestead

This historic home, located 30km south of Canberra, dates from 1859 and is classified by the National Trust. The homestead has lovely gardens, tea-rooms, a gift shop and a fine collection of Sidney Nolan paintings.
Open: Tuesday to Sunday 10am–4pm.

Namadgi National Park

In the southwest section of the ACT this park offers some dramatic scenery and is often snow-covered in winter. There is good bushwalking and horse riding here, as well as picnic and camping facilities.

Tidbinbilla Nature Reserve

This 5,000-hectare site southwest of Canberra is a reserve for indigenous flora and fauna: it also contains several walking trails and picnic sites.

NEARBY

Two small NSW towns which are within easy reach of the ACT are Braidwood and Bungendore. The former dates from the 1830s and is one of the state's most historic villages, while Bungendore is famous for its colonial-style shops and the excellent Carrington Hotel.

A memorial to Captain Cook

Inland

*T*his rather general term covers those parts of New South Wales, excluding the outback, that are not within easy reach of Sydney, or on the coast. This vast region is the heartland of the state – small country towns, huge tracts of fertile farming land, and distinctively Australian scenery of plains and hills, gum trees and waterways. The area also contains many beautiful national parks which protect this priceless heritage. The following are some highlights of NSW's inland.

BATHURST AND ORANGE

West of the Blue Mountains and on the far side of the Great Dividing Range, this area was first settled in the early 1800s and provided much-needed farming land for the desperate Sydney community.

BATHURST

Governor Macquarie personally selected the site for Bathurst in 1815, to create the country's first inland town. The excellent farming land here led to rapid settlement, and the present day city is still at the centre of a prosperous agricultural region. Bathurst is 200km northwest of Sydney and contains many fine old buildings, such as the 1880 Courthouse, which attest to its importance. The city has a good art gallery and visitors can also see the modest home of Ben Chifley, a former Prime Minister of Australia.
Bathurst Regional Art Gallery. Open: Monday to Friday 10am–4pm, weekend 1pm–4pm.
Ben Chifley's Home. Open: Monday to Saturday 2pm–4pm, Sunday 10am–noon.

ORANGE

This attractive city, to the northwest of Bathurst, flourished during the goldrush era of the 1850s and has continued to prosper through agriculture. Many fine

buildings here include the excellent Regional Art Gallery, Civic Theatre and Historical Museum.
Orange Regional Art Gallery. Open: Tuesday to Saturday 11am–5pm, Sunday 2pm–5pm.
Orange Historical Museum. Open: Saturday and Sunday 2pm–5pm.

NEW ENGLAND AREA

This is another important agricultural region, some 540km north of Sydney.

ARMIDALE

Armidale is one of the state's most attractive inland settlements. Set high within the rolling New England hills, the city is full of parks and gardens which are particularly lovely in the cool of autumn. The University of New England is located here, off Elizabeth Drive, and Armidale also boasts two cathedrals and several churches. Don't miss the excellent New England Regional Art Museum, which contains many fine examples of Australian landscapes and contemporary paintings. Three national parks – New England, Cathedral Rock and Oxley Wild Rivers – are all within easy reach of the city.
University of New England. Tel: (067) 73 2099. Open: by prior arrangement only.
New England Regional Art Museum.

*Open: Monday to Saturday 10am–5pm,
Sunday 1pm–5pm.*

TAMWORTH

Southwest of Armidale, this city is
known as Australia's country music
capital: the popular, 11-day Country
Music Festival is held here each January.
This area, too, is a prosperous
agricultural region, noted for its sheep
and wheat. Interesting buildings to see
include a good art gallery.
*Tamworth City Art Gallery. Open:
Monday to Friday 10am–5pm, Saturday
9am–11.30am.*

THE SOUTH

To the west of Canberra and southwest
from Sydney lies yet another fertile
agricultural region which contains a
number of substantial townships.

WAGGA WAGGA

This Aboriginal name often fascinates
visitors – it means 'many crows' and is
believed to be an imitation of their call.
This large city has a population of
around 37,000 and is located on the
Murrumbidgee River. The area supports
a wide range of agricultural pursuits and
visitors will enjoy the city's botanic
gardens and zoo, art gallery and
museum. There are several wineries
here, and other historic towns such as
Temora, Junee and Gundagai are worth
a visit. Nearby Griffith (see Wine-
producing Areas), should also be
included in your itinerary.
*Botanic Gardens and Zoo. Open: daily
9.30am–5pm.*
*Wagga Wagga City Art Gallery. Open:
Monday to Wednesday 11am–5pm,
Sunday 2pm–5pm. Admission fee.*
Wineries. Open: daily 9am–5pm.

WARRUMBUNGLE NATIONAL PARK

This remarkable region, 490km
northwest of Sydney, deserves special
mention. Ancient volcanic activity has
created a wonderful landscape of jagged
lava peaks and domes which rise
dramatically from the surrounding
plains. The area is marvellous for
walking, rock-climbing and bird-
watching, and the scenery here is among
the finest in eastern Australia.

COONABARABRAN

This pleasant town of around 3,000
people is the gateway to the national
park. Near by is the fascinating Siding
Spring Observatory: a world-renowned
astronomical observatory complex.
*Siding Spring Observatory. Open: daily
9am–4pm. Admission fee.*

OTHER PLACES OF INTEREST

Many inland towns, such as Parkes,
Forbes and Dubbo in the mid-west, and
Moree, Tenterfield, Glen Innes and
Inverell in the north are all interesting
places to visit – if you have the time.

Armidale's delightful Post Office

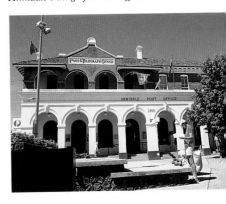

Islands

*T*here are few people who are not captivated by islands, and New South Wales is fortunate to have two remarkable island destinations off its coast. Both Lord Howe and Norfolk are not only scenically beautiful, they also have unique and fascinating histories. Access to both islands is by air: from Sydney to Norfolk, and to Lord Howe from Sydney and Port Macquarie.

LORD HOWE ISLAND

This tiny but spectacular island is 700km northeast of Sydney. Lord Howe was listed as a World Heritage area in 1982 owing to its soaring volcanic peaks, the world's most southerly coral reef, exceptional birdlife and general scenic beauty. The island has a population of around 300: it is 11km long and 2.8km across at its widest point. Lord Howe was first sighted and declared uninhabited in 1788, and named after the First Lord of the Admiralty. Settlement began in 1834 and the island became a port for ships *en route* to Norfolk Island.

Whaling ships also called in here and today the Lord Howe population includes many descendants of an American whaler named Thompson.

Visitor numbers are strictly limited, making Lord Howe a perfect, uncrowded holiday destination. Aquatic opportunities abound – boating, magnificent scuba diving, swimming and snorkelling. The island's 37km of shore contains a number of lovely beaches for those who just want to relax. Boat tours are available for fishing, coral reef viewing and general sightseeing.

Bushwalkers enjoy the challenge of plodding to the top of Mounts Gower (875m) and Lidgbird (777m) for the magnificent views. Cycling is also a popular activity, made more pleasant by the fact that there are very few cars on

The Royal Engineer Office, Norfolk Island

the island. The bicycle is actually the main means of transportation for visitors and locals alike. This is also a bird-watching paradise; 130 species have been recorded here and there are many offshore bird colonies which you can visit.

NORFOLK ISLAND

This isolated and much larger island, 1,600km east of Sydney, was first discovered by Captain Cook in 1774 during his second voyage round the world. Norfolk has had a grim but fascinating history – its isolation led to the development of a brutal and much feared penal settlement for the New South Wales colony here at various times between 1788 and 1855. The island later became the home of the Pitcairn Islanders, including descendants of the *Bounty* mutineers, who were moved here in 1856.

Norfolk is less sub-tropical in appearance than Lord Howe and is characterised by its Norfolk Island pine trees and grasslands. The coastline contains some lovely sandy beaches and there are a number of good bushwalks on the island.

Today, Norfolk Island supports around 2,000 people, most of whom are engaged in tourism and agriculture, particularly cattle breeding. There are still many Pitcairn descendants here, who speak 'Norfolk', an intriguing mixture of Tahitian and English. The island no longer belongs to NSW but is a Territory of Australia, with no income or sales taxes! It is also famous for its kentia palm and Norfolk pine seedlings, which are exported to many countries.

KINGSTON

The historic Georgian settlement of

Norfolk Island's attractive coastline

Kingston contains many buildings from the second convict era between 1826 and 1855. Highlights include the old Military Barracks (1826–32), the new Barracks (1836), the Gaol and the cemetery with its fascinating headstones in memory of convicts and Pitcairn Islanders. The town also contains a Bounty Folk Museum and St Barnabas' Chapel, built in 1880 of stone from the penal ruins.

Kingston Historic Buildings and Bounty Folk Museum. Open: daily 10am–5pm.

The Murray River

*T*he Murray is Australia's largest and most important river. It rises in the Great Dividing Range and flows for over 2,500km, forming the majority of the border between Victoria and New South Wales. From Wentworth, in far west NSW, the river continues into South Australia and turns south, finally entering Lake Alexandrina and the ocean. The river is less important for transport today, but in the 19th-century heyday of river steamers, the waterway was a vital lifeline to the three states. The Murray is still agriculturally important, however, and is used extensively for irrigation. There are many historic port towns on the Murray which owe their existence both to agriculture and the waterway's presence.

ALBURY

Located on the River Murray and across the border from its Victorian sister city of Wodonga, Albury is southern NSW's largest centre. This city of around 37,000 people is at the heart of a large and fertile agricultural region and is also a National Growth Centre, the aim of which has been to encourage the decentralisation of industry from major state capitals. Consequently, Albury and Wodonga have numerous industrial concerns, but also much to interest the visitor.

The city contains many historic buildings and is famed for its attractive parks and gardens. The surrounding region has several interesting old towns such as Culcairn, Henty and Holbrook and was once the haunt of bushrangers like Mad Dan Morgan, who terrorised locals and travellers alike during the 1860s. Man-made Lake Hume, just a few kilometres away, is an aquatic playground which attracts many anglers, yachting fans and waterskiers.

COROWA

This small Murray town developed as a port during the 1850s and has an important place in national history. It was here, in 1893, that a major conference on the federation of Australia's states was held – the town has an interesting Federation Museum. The area is important for its wheat and wool production and there are also several wineries. Visitors can take river cruises, explore the town and its 19th-century buildings, and cross the Murray to visit northern Victoria's famous Rutherglen wine region.

Federation Museum. Open: weekends 2pm–5pm.

MOAMA

Moama is across the river from the more important town of Echuca, and has long been connected with that historic Victorian settlement. A punt river crossing was established here in the 1840s and the site grew up as a cattle market town. When Echuca became the terminus of the Melbourne railway line in 1864, the area developed rapidly, becoming Australia's largest inland port. Moama is now a popular holiday centre with some pleasant campsites and picnic spots along the banks of the Murray River.

THE RIVERINA

This is the name given to the northern borderlands of the River Murray – a fertile region which is one of the state's most important agricultural districts. Crops such as rice, vegetables and citrus fruits are grown here and the region supports many cattle and merino sheep properties. Corowa is in this area and other small, historic towns such as Jerilderie, Finley and Deniliquin are interesting to visit.

Wentworth, led to a decline in the river trade, but the town still prospered in its role as an agricultural settlement. Nowadays, Wentworth is important as the centre of the region's irrigation scheme, and the heart of a citrus and avocado-growing area.

Visitors are drawn to the town's river location, as well as its many historic buildings – the Gaol, for example, dates from 1881, while St John's Church was built in the 1870s. Other attractions

WENTWORTH

Wentworth's position at the junction of the Murray and Darling Rivers, close to the South Australian border, long made it the hub of river trade for the three states.

During the river steamer days of the 1800s, Wentworth was a busy port, handling goods of all descriptions, but especially wool. The coming of the railway to the region, but not to

An ideal way to explore the Murray River area is a leisurely steamer trip

include river cruises on the Murray and Darling, and visits to nearby picturesque villages and the Stanley Winery at Buronga.

Old Wentworth Gaol. Open: daily 10am–5pm.
Stanley Winery. Open: Monday to Saturday 9am–5pm, Sunday noon–5pm.

The North Coast

*F*rom Sydney, the north coast of NSW stretches over 900km to the Queensland border, just beyond Tweed Heads. The region abounds with beautiful surf beaches, lakes, rivers, spectacular inland scenery and small coastal towns. Understandably, it is one of the state's favourite holiday playgrounds.

FAR NORTH
Ballina
Located on an island in the Richmond River, Ballina is a commercial fishing and ship-building port, and also a popular holiday resort. The area has some excellent beaches and town highlights include a lighthouse, wildlife sanctuary and river cruises.
South Ballina Wildlife Sanctuary. Open: Wednesday to Sunday 10am–5.30pm. Admission fee.

Byron Bay
Undoubtedly the gem of the entire NSW coast, Byron Bay is, so far, an unspoilt paradise. Cape Byron, with its distinctive lighthouse, is Australia's most easterly point and is surrounded by some of the state's most beautiful beaches. This is a popular surfing and watersports town, and 'Byron' is also the home of many alternative lifestylers who appreciate the region's spectacular natural beauty and calm atmosphere.

Tweed Heads
This is NSW's northernmost town and is linked closely with Queensland's Coolangatta, just a few kilometres away. The beach life here is superb and the area is close to Queensland's over-developed, but somehow incredibly popular, Gold Coast, with its ritzy hotels, casino and thriving nightlife.

MID NORTH
Coffs Harbour
This harbour and port town, with its fine nearby beaches, has developed into a popular holiday region with excellent tourist facilities, including some top-class resorts. The surfing is good, and 'Coffs' is also a well-known yachting centre. The region is semi-tropical – bananas are grown here, and the nearby Dorrigo National Park is a haven of rainforest, waterfalls and lush vegetation. Inland from Coffs, white-water rafting is a popular activity on the Nymboida River.

Grafton
Although some 65km inland, at the mouth of the Clarence River, Grafton is another favourite holiday destination. This pleasant city is at the centre of a dairying and sugar cane-growing region and originally developed as a port. Visitors will enjoy activities such as river cruising on the majestic Clarence; there are also several national parks near by and the city contains many historic buildings.
Grafton Historic Buildings. Open: most are open 10am–5pm.

Port Macquarie
Port Macquarie, 420km from Sydney, was founded in 1821 as a convict outpost and is the north coast's most historic town. Nowadays, it is a busy resort and the centre of a well-patronised holiday

No prizes for guessing the major crop here

area. To the north, Kempsey, on the Macleay River, and South West Rocks and Crescent Head with their fine, unspoilt beaches, are other attractions which are worth visiting while in the area.

MYALL LAKES / PORT STEPHENS REGION

Further south, there are yet more beautiful beaches and resorts within easy reach of Sydney.

Myall Lakes National Park

This extraordinary region, 236km north of the state capital, offers the best of both worlds: golden beaches and surf, and a chain of sparkling freshwater lakes. The Myall Lakes region is a holiday paradise: fishing, boating, camping, swimming, surfing, canoeing and bird-watching are all popular activities. For those not camping, the nearby towns of Bulahdelah and the quaintly named Tea Gardens are good places to stay. To the north, Taree is an attractive market town on the banks of the Manning River and is the access point for good beaches and oceanside Crowdy Bay National Park.

Port Stephens

To the south of Myall Lakes, the Port Stephens peninsula is another lovely holiday region. The peninsula includes the towns of Nelson Bay and Shoal Bay, and a 25km harbour which offers terrific aquatic opportunities. Despite development, the area is largely unspoilt and has some of the north coast's most attractive white, sandy beaches.

INLAND

Although the coast and beaches are obviously the main attraction, the region's hinterland is worth visiting too. The semi-tropical climate has led to areas of lush rainforest, such as in the Dorrigo National Park, and the slopes and rivers of the Great Dividing Range provide many opportunities for canoeing, rafting and bushwalking.

The Outback

*F*ar away from the coast, the Outback presents a very different side of New South Wales. This is the land of heat, dust and drought – and some fascinating and often bizarre history.

CORNER COUNTRY

This area, at the junction of the NSW, Queensland and South Australia borders, is the state's wildest and most remote region.

Camerons Corner

This is the godforsaken spot, marked by a white post, where the borders of the three states meet. From here it is possible to see the famous Dingo Fence, which has the distinction of being the world's longest fence – it runs the width of the continent, from the Gulf of Carpentaria to the Indian Ocean.

Sturt National Park

This vast, semi-desert park contains hectares of sand dunes, rocky plains and normally dry lake beds which are sometimes, surprisingly, full of water. The region is home to a wide variety of wildlife such as kangaroos, emus, many types of lizard and wonderful birdlife. After the occasional heavy rain, the desert comes alive with a proliferation of attractive and unusual wildflowers.

Tibooburra

At 1,505km from Sydney, the small, dry and dusty town of Tibooburra is the state's most isolated settlement, and usually the hottest. The ultimate outback NSW town developed as a gold mining centre during the 1880s and contains several National Trust classified buildings.

NORTH
Bourke

Despite its very definite outback location – a popular Australian expression, which implies that this is the last outpost of civilisation, is 'Back o' Bourke' – this town is on the Darling River and has long been an important wool port. The first building here was erected in 1835, and during the 1860s and 1870s the town became the centre of a major wool producing district. Irrigation from the Darling has also permitted the growth of cotton and citrus fruits. It is a fascinating town of around 3,500 people, containing many historic buildings, and has great appeal for visitors.

Lightning Ridge

Lightning Ridge is all about opals. The fields here are the most important in NSW and are particularly famous for their highly valued black varieties. Some 1,000 people of over 30 nationalities base themselves here, in extreme weather conditions and with artesian bore water as their only supply, to mine the fields. Visitors can tour various mines and are permitted to 'fossick' (prospect) for the gems.
Opal Mines. Open: daily 9am–5pm. Admission fee.

SOUTH
Balranald

A small, rather isolated town on the Murrumbidgee River, 857km west of

Sydney, Balranald is the centre of a vast sheep, cattle and wheat-growing area and the base from which to explore Mungo – one of the state's most important national parks.

Mungo National Park

This ancient and now dry lakebed area lies within the Willandra Lakes World Heritage Region, designated as such because of its significant Aboriginal heritage value. Evidence has been found that Aboriginal people lived here as long as 40,000 years ago. The sparsely vegetated park contains some weird and wonderful dune scenery and has an interesting variety of bird and animal life.

WEST
Broken Hill

By far the state's largest outback settlement, Broken Hill is a thriving mining city of some 26,000 people. Silver was discovered here in 1883 and, unlike many outback boom towns, the mining industry has survived. Today, silver, lead and zinc are still mined in large quantities and the city was the birthplace of Broken Hill Proprietary Limited (BHP), Australia's biggest company. There is an interesting art gallery and some mines welcome visitors. The state's Royal Flying Doctor service headquarters are also open to the public.

Nearby attractions include dramatic Kinchega National Park, Lake Menindee and Silverton, a booming silver mining settlement in the 1880s, but now a fascinating ghost town.

Broken Hill Art Gallery. Open: daily 10am–5pm. Admission fee.
Delprats Underground Mine. Open: tours Monday to Friday 10.30am, Saturday 2pm. Admission fee.
North Mine Surface Tour. Open: tours Monday to Friday 10am. Admission fee.
Royal Flying Doctor Service Headquarters. Open: daily 9am–5pm.

White Cliffs

White Cliffs is another small opal-mining settlement. Most of the population live underground to combat both the fierce summer heat, and, ironically, the cold in winter. Visitors can stay in an underground motel and also tour the nearby Solar Power Station.

Solar Power Station. Open: daily for tours 2pm. Admission fee.

Wilcannia

This town on the Darling River was once one of NSW's largest inland ports, but Wilcannia today is a sleepy pastoral town which contains many interesting buildings built during the 1870s and the 1890s era.

The Palace Hotel, Broken Hill

40,000 Years of Aboriginal History

The discovery of Aboriginal remains dating back some 40,000 years in NSW's Mungo National Park is sufficient evidence to prove that this land really does belong to the Aboriginal people. Until the 18th century, native Australians lived an isolated and contented life: these nomadic people hunted, fished and foraged, while respecting the land and its bounty. The coming of the white man changed this scenario dramatically – disease, destruction and racial hatred followed. In Sydney, for example, within three years of the arrival of the First Fleet, the Aboriginal population was reduced by two-thirds through smallpox, influenza, accidents and violent death.

Today, as then, this displaced people are often regarded as an inferior race. Sadly, most Aborigines live either in run-down Sydney suburbs, or as fringe dwellers of outback towns like Wilcannia, Broken Hill and Bourke, where race relations are often strained, and existing problems are exacerbated by over-indulgence in alcohol.

This tragic picture belies the fascinating spiritual and cultural life of the Aborigine. Many people have heard of the Dreamtime. This is a system of beliefs – which represents man, animals, nature and the land bound inseparably together – that forms the basis of Aboriginal life, culture and heritage. To the Aborigine, the land is sacred, and this viewpoint is perhaps best expressed in the fascinating art of the indigenous Australian people.

Aboriginal art, past and present, may seem to the casual observer to be merely a series of attractive, earthy-hued patterns. In fact, each bark painting, rock engraving or painted didgeridoo tells a complex story of campsites, paths in the desert, animals, spirits and sacred sites.

Visitors who are interested in Aboriginal culture should not miss Sydney's Australian Museum, and the National Gallery in Canberra. Out in the field there are some wonderful rock engravings in Sydney's Ku-ring-gai Chase National Park and, further afield, sites such as Mungo and Kinchega (near Broken Hill) national parks contain many remnants of the Aboriginal lifestyle that is, for the most part, a thing of the past.

Decorated graves in Victoria

Aborigine warrior with boomerang

Boomerang practice - Coranderrk 1889

Traditional kangaroo hunt

The Snowy Mountains

*T*he extreme south of New South Wales contains some surprises for the visitor. Many people are not even aware that it snows in Australia; most are surprised to discover that it is possible to ski here. Although the Snowy Mountains are low in elevation by world standards, the skiing is excellent in winter, and in summer the region is perfect for bushwalking or horse riding.

The Snowy Mountains in summer

Skiing

The ski season runs from June to October, with the snow generally at its best from late July to mid-September. Downhill skiing is possible at Thredbo, Perisher Valley, Smiggin Holes and the region's other four resorts, and the sparsely populated area is also particularly good for cross-country skiing. Mount Selwyn, Charlotte's Pass and Guthega are the best areas for this activity. All resorts have good standards of accommodation and full equipment hire facilities. Skiers of all abilities will find suitable conditions here.

ADAMINABY REGION

This area is in the northern section of the park and is reached from Cooma. Adaminaby is a relatively new town, created in 1957 to replace the original which was drowned when Lake Eucumbene was created for the purposes of irrigation and hydro-electric power. Near by is what remains of Kiandra, an old gold rush town and the birthplace of Australian skiing which began here as early as the 1860s. The Yarrangobilly Caves are also worth a visit: there are 50 or so caves here, many of which are open to the public. Horse riding is a popular holiday activity in the area.

Yarrangobilly Caves. Open: daily 9am–5pm. Admission fee.

COOMA

Cooma is around 400km from Sydney and its position at the junctions of the Monaro and Snowy Mountains highways makes it the gateway to the region. For most of the year this is a quiet farming town but in winter, skiers descend in their hordes and pack the many ski-hire shops, restaurants and hotels.

JINDABYNE

This attractive town on the shores of Lake Jindabyne is the nearest to the mountains and is another winter ski centre. The man-made lake is part of the Snowy Mountains Hydro-Electric Scheme and in summer it is an excellent spot for fishing, boating and waterskiing. It's also possible to go white-water rafting in the area.

KOSCIUSKO NATIONAL PARK

The 629,000 hectares of this national park includes the Snowy Mountains and some of Australia's most spectacular scenery. The park stretches along the Great Dividing Range and at its heart lies 2,228m Mount Kosciusko, the continent's highest peak. The mountain may not be high by world standards, but the dramatic scenery more than compensates. The park contains rugged moorland, glacial lakes, caves and the headwaters of the Murray River, Australia's largest waterway. Although covered with snow in winter, the region looks totally different in spring and early summer, as grasses, wildflowers and many varieties of eucalyptus tree come alive. The birdlife is prolific: there are more than 200 species here, and the abundant wildlife includes kangaroos, possums and wombats.

The park's main Visitor Centre at Sawpit Creek (on the road from Jindabyne) has excellent information on the region, as well as displays on various aspects of the park.
Kosciusko National Park Visitor Centre. Open: daily 8.30am–4.30pm.

PERISHER VALLEY

This valley, on the northern side of Mount Kosciusko, has two very popular ski resorts: Perisher and Smiggin Holes. The facilities here are excellent, with

Sunrise at Perisher Valley

many ski-lifts and a good variety of skiing conditions that will suit everyone from total beginners to experts.

THREDBO

Located in a narrow valley on the southern side of Mount Kosciusko, Thredbo is a pretty European alpine-style village which provides immediate access to the ski fields. Chairlifts criss-cross the slopes – one of which takes skiers to the top of Crackenback, 1,960m up the mountain. In summer, the resort offers bushwalking, tennis, fishing, horse riding and mountain biking. There are some excellent bars and restaurants here and the resort is considered to be the most up-market in the region.

On the shores of Lake Jindabyne

The South Coast

*D*espite the fact that the south coast has beaches and inland scenery to rival that of the north, there has been little development here, and the region is far less commercial and crowded.

FAR SOUTH COAST

This remote corner of New South Wales, near the Victorian border, is truly a hidden gem. Lovely beaches are the norm, and the area is never over-crowded.

BEN BOYD NATIONAL PARK

Named after an early settler of the region, this park stretches along the coast to both the north and south of Eden. It includes some beautiful beaches and geologically interesting coastline, and offers excellent fishing, swimming and bushwalking opportunities.

EDEN

The most southerly town in NSW, 498km from Sydney, this is the south coast's main port, which developed from the 1800s whaling industry. Today, fishing is the major activity here and tourism also brings an income to many of the locals.

MERIMBULA

The small resort of Merimbula has more than just beautiful beaches: it is in an attractive position at the mouth of the Merimbula River and is backed by a lake. Pambula, to the south, is another unspoiled beach resort, which is popular with surfers.

JERVIS BAY AND ULLADULLA

This south coast region begins just 180km from Sydney, and contains Jervis Bay, one of the state's most idyllic spots.

JERVIS BAY

Part of this vast, almost circular bay is, like the Australian Capital Territory, classified as federal land and contains

Fishing near Narooma's oyster beds

HMAS *Creswell*, the prestigious Australian Naval College. Most of the bay is virtually undeveloped, with a few small towns such as Huskisson and Vincentia catering for the needs of visitors. The famous beaches here are startlingly white; the sea is a perfect blue and the area attracts many swimmers, anglers and scuba divers. Much of the surrounding land is regarded as sacred by the Aboriginal community.

ULLADULLA
Ulladulla is quite a contrast to the unspoiled Jervis Bay area but, despite its development, the town is surrounded by some excellent beaches and camping spots. It has been a large fishing port since the 1930s and the region also has several attractive lakes, heathland and wildflower reserves. Budawang National Park, a marvellous bushwalking area, is near by.

MID SOUTH COAST
BATEMANS BAY
Batemans Bay, named by Captain Cook in 1770, is the closest beach resort to Canberra – 150km away – and is very popular with these inland city dwellers. The pleasant town and port are at the mouth of the Clyde River and the region is well known for its oysters and crayfish.

DURRAS
To the north of Batemans Bay, Durras is a much quieter spot, which has thankfully experienced very little development. The lovely coast is surrounded by forest and backed by lagoon-like Lake Durras. The area contains an award-winning caravan and camping park and is perfect for the visitor who prefers to get away from the crowd.

MORUYA
South of Batemans Bay, Moruya is a quiet, historic town 6km inland on the Moruya River. It dates from 1850 and the region was once famous for its fine granite, which was used in the construction of the Sydney Harbour Bridge pylons.

To the south, the Tuross Head peninsula has some fine beaches, and Deua National Park is good for bush-walking and caving.

NAROOMA
There are yet more wonderful beaches here, and the area is very popular with fishermen. The small town is centred around oyster farming, fishing and the timber industry and there are some interesting places near by. To the south, Bermagui is a lovely resort town, while historic Tilba is a National Trust classified village. There is also a winery in the region.
Tilba Historic Village. Open: most buildings daily 10am–5pm.
Tilba Valley Winery. Open: Monday to Saturday 10am–5pm.

INLAND
The south coast hinterland is best described as pastoral. Most of the scenery here is more gentle than that of the north, and towns such as Bega and Nowra have grown up around agricultural pursuits. Nowra is a centre for trips to Jervis Bay and the Southern Highlands, while Bega, inland from Merimbula, is an important dairying region; the local cheese is particularly good.

There are many rugged national parks in the hinterland: Deua and Wadbilliga (near Bega) are particularly worth a visit.

Wine-producing Areas

*A*ustralia produces some excellent red, white and sparkling wines, many of which are from New South Wales. In addition to the attractions of sampling the fruit of the vine, the state's wine areas are scenic regions which have much more to offer the visitor.

Wineries in all regions are generally open daily for tastings and tours from 9am to 5pm.

A selection of Hunter Valley's wines

HUNTER VALLEY

This wide valley, which follows the course of the Hunter River, is the state's most famous wine-producing region, and is located to the northwest of Newcastle. It is divided into two distinct areas.

Lower Hunter

Cessnock, 183km from Sydney, is the centre of the Lower Hunter region. The city was founded on the coal-mining industry, but the wineries are also a major concern. This area produces some of the state's best wines: McWilliams Mount Pleasant, Lindemans, Hungerford Hill, Tyrrells and Brokenwood are some of the 30 or so wineries that are located here. A drive around Cessnock, Pokolbin, Rothbury and the historic village of Broke will take in most of these establishments.

Upper Hunter
A further 100km to the northwest, this is a smaller, newer and less visited wine area than the Lower Hunter, but some very good wines are produced here. The town of Muswellbrook is the centre of this region, which is also known for its coal mining and agriculture. The best wineries here are Arrowfield and Rosemount Estate.

MUDGEE
Although less visited by tourists and wine fanciers than the Hunter Valley region, Mudgee produces some excellent wines and is also a picturesque area to visit. The first graziers arrived here in 1822 and the town is one of the oldest in the state, dating from 1837. Many of its historic buildings are classified under the National Trust.

Mudgee is set in a wide, fertile valley, where wine has been produced since German migrants introduced the industry in the 1820s. There are around 18 wineries in the area, including Craigmoor Wines, established in 1858, Montrose, and the small, but excellent, Seldom Seen Winery.

SOUTHERN WINERIES
Griffith
Wine is also produced in southern NSW, particularly around the Griffith area, west of Sydney and Canberra, where vines have been tended since 1913. The Hunter Valley-based McWilliams have an establishment here, and other small, family-run wineries include De Bortoli and Miranda.

WINES OF NEW SOUTH WALES
Australian wines are deservedly gaining an international reputation, and many of these are produced in New South Wales. There have been vineyards in NSW since the 1820s, but it was not until 150 years later that wine became widely popular and the industry really developed its district yet varied styles.

There are some excellent red wines, coming under names such as Cabernet Sauvignon, Shiraz and Pinot Noir. Good whites include Chardonnay, Semillon, Riesling, Chablis, white Burgundy and sweet, Sauterne-style dessert wines. The names might sound European, but the wines are very definitely Australian: reds are often rich and full-bodied and the light whites, such as Chardonnay, are delightful. Many sparkling, champagne-type wines are also made, and Italian-style Lambrusco is produced in the Griffith region.

Look for popular labels such as Rosemount Estate, Lindemans, Tyrrells, Montrose, Rothbury Estate, McWilliams, Wyndham Estate and Hungerford Hill. Some good, lesser-known, wines are made by Seldom Seen in Mudgee, Griffith's de Bortoli, and Lake's Folly and Simon Whitlam in the Hunter Valley.

VICTORIAN WINERIES
From the Albury/Wodonga area, in the state's far south, the famous wineries of northeast Victoria are easily accessible and definitely worth a visit.

Getting away from it all

Unlike the world's other major cities, getting away from it all in Sydney is a simple affair. Those who choose to can travel west to the Blue Mountains, north to the Central Coast or south to the Highlands, but it's not absolutely necessary to do so. Within the Sydney metropolitan area, and indeed within the central region, there are many lovely spots in which to relax and take time out from the hard work of sightseeing.

Enjoy a picnic overlooking the harbour; cruise the waterways in a houseboat; lie on a sandy beach, or visit a flower-bedecked garden. Many of

The glorious sweep of Avalon Beach

these places are relatively crowded at weekends, but remember that Sydney's population is a mere 3.6 million – there's plenty of room for not too many people.

Outside the city region there are more wonderful possibilities for escaping the hustle and bustle. New South Wales has countless lovely beaches, waterways, national parks and areas of unspoiled bush to enjoy. There are many opportunities to get close to the continent's amazing wildlife and, if your interest lies in adventure, rather than relaxation, you'll be delighted at the available prospects.

UNCROWDED BEACHES

If soaking up the summer sun beside glittering water is your idea of heaven, there are plenty of locations at which to indulge yourself. Many beaches are uncrowded during the week, and others require just a little more effort to reach.

CITY REGION
Cronulla

For those prepared for a fair walk along Sydney's longest and most southerly beach, there are plenty of unpopulated spots to enjoy. Cronulla stretches for 10km and is a haven for surfers.
Train to Cronulla, then bus 66 or 67.

Ku-ring-gai Chase National Park

This bushland area, to the north of the city, borders on the Pittwater and Cowan Creek waterways and contains many small, secluded beaches. The best of these are reached on foot: examples are Flint and Steel Beach and America Bay on West Head. Full details are

Congwong Bay, near Bare Island

available from the National Parks and Wildlife Service. Another good beach, but more crowded, is at The Basin, reached by ferry from Palm Beach.

Nude beaches

Although seldom empty, Sydney's two nude beaches are another option. They are Lady Jane at Watsons Bay and Reef Beach, near Balgowlah Heights.

NORTH COAST
Byron Bay

This lovely region has stretches of surf beaches that contain plenty of remote and quiet spots.

CENTRAL COAST

The waterways of the Central Coast offer many small, uncrowded beaches to explore. Brisbane Water National Park contains spots such as Patonga and Pearl Beach, while the neighbouring Bouddi National Park offers McMasters, Kilcare and Little beaches.

SOUTH COAST

Jervis Bay

This vast bay, south of Wollongong, contains beautiful Hyams Beach, which is believed to have the whitest sand in the world! The bay has many other beaches, most of which are fairly empty, all of them lapped by clear blue water. The area is also very popular with scuba divers.

Royal National Park

Just a few kilometres to the south of the city limits, the Royal's 21km coastline contains numerous surf-washed beaches. Many of these can become busy in summer, but it's always possible to avoid the crowds. A good walk in either direction along the main beach, Garie, will almost guarantee a quiet spot. If you're interested in bushwalking, there are several lovely beaches within the park that are accessible only by foot: Marley, Little Marley and Curracurrang are some examples. In the far south, Werrong is not only secluded, it is an authorised nude beach.

Boating

*P*erhaps the best means of getting away from it all is by taking to the water. There is little to compare with the freedom of exploring the state's many lovely waterways, and even sleeping on board your chosen craft for a few nights. Whether in busy Sydney Harbour, cruising a remote corner of the Hawkesbury River, or meandering along the broad River Murray, New South Wales has some wonderful boating opportunities. See the **Practical Guide** for details of boat-hire operators.

THE MURRAY RIVER
In the south of the state, the mighty Murray offers boating with a difference. From towns such as Wentworth and Moama it is possible to cruise the river on paddleboats from a bygone era. Houseboats can also be hired from various points along the river if you prefer an independent experience of the Murray. Whichever craft you choose, boating is the perfect way to explore this uniquely Australian region, with its meandering river, varied gum trees, stark red cliffs and wonderful birdlife.

THE MYALL LAKES
The Myall Lakes region, north of Newcastle, is one of the state's best boating venues. These tranquil lakes, which comprise a third of the national park, are a perfect location for canoeing or pottering about in a small boat. There are innumerable inlets and small bays to explore, and the area is home to a wide variety of wildlife. The lakes are also great for sailboarding and sailing and it is possible to hire houseboats here.

PITTWATER AND THE HAWKESBURY RIVER
Sydney's Pittwater and the neighbouring waterways of the Hawkesbury, Broken Bay and Cowan Creek are an ideal

Speedboat fun on Manly Beach

location for boating. The eastern shore of Pittwater is developed, but much of the area belongs to Ku-ring-gai Chase National Park and there are hundreds of isolated spots to explore. Yachts and cruisers can be hired from Brooklyn and Bobbin Head.

The region is also great for houseboating. These craft sleep several people, are easy to manage, and there is no better way of seeing the wonderful scenery of Ku-ring-gai and the nearby Marramarra and Dharug national parks. Houseboats can also be taken up-river towards the Richmond/Windsor region to explore the farmland, small towns and pretty creeks of this area.

PORT STEPHENS
The beautiful waterways of this area,

between Newcastle and the Myall Lakes, are another perfect boating venue. Here you can hire easily-handled houseboats of all sizes, or yachts and motor cruisers if you prefer.

SYDNEY HARBOUR

Whether you take an inexpensive ferry trip, or splash out and hire a yacht for the day, Sydney Harbour is the perfect place to go boating. It's one of those places where, even if you're on a crowded ferry, you still feel as though you are a million miles away from city life.

There are many ways to experience the harbour. Ferries are fun – especially if you take the long Manly trip, or just cruise around on the shorter Neutral Bay or Mosman runs. Head west, under the bridge, to Balmain or Hunters Hill to see a different aspect of the harbour. You can join a cruise which provides an informative commentary, or sail on the *Bounty*, one of the city's tall ships. For those with some boating experience, the best option is to hire a self-drive yacht or motor cruiser and get away from the tourist spots.

The harbour has thousands of attractive bays, nooks and crannies to

The ferry John Cadman II *at work*

explore, and it is not impossible, even at weekends, to find an almost deserted patch of beach which can be reached only by boat.

Pittwater's famous Palm Beach

Outdoor Adventures

*T*he excellent climate, beautiful scenery and largely unspoiled countryside mean that New South Wales offers many opportunities for outdoor adventures. This is by far the best way to explore the state's wilderness areas and to get away from the normal tourist trails. It is advisable to arrange most of the following activities through one of the many travel operators who specialise in adventure, although bushwalking, for example, is easy to organise on your own. The National Parks and Wildlife Service are particularly helpful in this regard and can be contacted on 585 6333. For details of operators see the **Practical Guide**.

BUSHWALKING

There is no better way to explore the state's beautiful bushland than on foot. The other advantage is that bushwalking requires little more equipment than strong footwear, a hat, a water bottle and a map. Virtually all of the state's wilderness areas are suitable for bushwalking and the many national parks are perfect destinations. Close to Sydney, the best opportunities are to be found in the Royal National Park, Blue Mountains, and around the Central Coast. Bushwalking is not advisable between January and March, however – high temperatures, the danger of bushfires and the presence of snakes make the activity better suited to the other nine months of the year.

CYCLING

Other than in Centennial Park, cycling in Sydney's crazy traffic is not advisable. Outside the city there are some fine tours in the Hunter Valley, and it's a great way to explore the wineries, or the gently rolling Southern Highlands, where a bicycle is ideal for the short distances between towns. Canberra, too, is an excellent cycling venue: there is a cycleway around Lake Burley Griffin and other rides which explore the Australian Capital Territory.

HORSE RIDING

If you want to ride in the city region, try Centennial Park, or one of the many riding schools in the Terrey Hills area, in the north of the metropolitan region – refer to the Yellow Pages phone book for ideas. The Blue Mountains and Southern Highlands are other good areas in which to ride and there are several operators here. The Snowy Mountains, however, offer the best opportunity for longer and more adventurous horseback exploration of the NSW bush.

ROCK SPORTS

The Blue Mountains are undoubtedly the best place to enjoy outdoor sports such as rock-climbing, abseiling and canyoning. The gorges and rocky outcrops here are perfect for anyone from beginners to the most accomplished climber. Other popular regions are in the Australian Capital Territory and the wonderful climber's paradise of the rugged Warrumbungle National Park, in the state's mid-north.

SAILBOARDING

Virtually anywhere on Sydney Harbour is perfect for sailboarding (windsurfing) and there are popular schools/equipment

Surf's up at North Beach, Cronulla

hire outlets at Rose Bay and The Spit. Otherwise, head over the bridge to Narrabeen Lakes, north of Manly. Further afield, the Myall Lakes region, north of Newcastle, is excellent.

SCUBA DIVING

This popular sport can be enjoyed at many lovely spots on the NSW coast, or even in Sydney Harbour itself. The best scuba locations are around Byron Bay and Coffs Harbour in the north, and in Jervis Bay, south of Sydney. Further afield, the reef around Lord Howe Island offers the state's most spectacular underwater environment.

SKIING

In winter (from June to October) the far south's Snowy Mountains become a skier's delight. The region has seven downhill ski resorts but, if you are interested in getting away from crowded slopes, there are many cross-country skiing opportunities on the tops of the ranges. This sport has become increasingly popular in Australia and is catered for by several expert tour companies.

WHITE-WATER RAFTING

If you really like adventure, book up with one of the many operators who specialise in white-water thrills and spills. The state's most suitable rafting rivers are in the Snowy Mountains region, and around Coffs Harbour.

Plenty of opportunities for hores riding

Parks and Gardens

*T*he Sydney area is full of green, open spaces and attractive formal gardens which are ideal spots in which to relax and take a break from sightseeing.

Lush vegetation in the Botanic Gardens

SYDNEY METROPOLITAN AREA
Bicentennial Park, Homebush
This 100-hectare park was opened in 1988 to commemorate Australia's Bicentenary. It features a large area of wetlands, cycling and walking paths and landscaped picnic and recreation areas. The park is close to the State Sports Centre's NSW Hall of Champions (see page 93).
Off Underwood Road, Homebush. Open: daily from sunrise to sunset. Train to Concord West.

Centennial Park, Paddington
The city's largest park becomes very busy at weekends, but its 220-hectare size means that it's always possible to find a somewhat secluded spot. Other than just lazing in the sun, or having a picnic beside the lake, the park offers cycling and horse riding opportunities (both forms of transport are available for hire).
Open: during daylight hours. Bus 380 to Oxford Street from Circular Quay.

Davidson Park State Recreation Area
Just 12km north of the city, Davidson Park covers a large portion of the upper reaches of Middle Harbour. Bush-walking and horse riding are possible here and there are also picnic areas, boat ramps and a shark-proof netted swimming area.
Open: during daylight hours. Access from Warringah Road, Forestville.

Lane Cove River State Recreation Area
This popular reserve is just a few kilometres northwest of the city and is based around the attractive Lane Cove River. Boating is the thing to do here: rowing boats or canoes can be hired for a small fee. There are many pleasant bushland picnic spots in this surprisingly unspoiled area of the city.
Open: during daylight hours. By car, or train to Chatswood Station, then a bus.

The Royal Botanic Gardens
The city's oldest and most scenic gardens are detailed on pages 52–3.

E G Waterhouse National Camellia Garden, Caringbah
Located in the otherwise residential southern suburb of Caringbah, this lovely landscaped garden specialises in camellias and azaleas. You could easily call in here after a visit to the Botany Bay area (see pages 82–3).
President Avenue, Caringbah. Open: daily 9.30am–4.30pm. Train to Caringbah, then walk or take a taxi.

THE BLUE MOUNTAINS
The Blue Mountains have long been famous for their lovely gardens – be sure to visit at least some of these when you tour the area. In addition to those listed, Blackheath has a famous rhododendron garden.

Mount Tomah Botanic Gardens
This bicentennial offshoot of the Royal Botanic Gardens is located on the scenic Bell's Line of Road, near Bilpin. The

Cacti flourish in ideal conditions

Native flowers provide dramatic colour

gardens specialise in cool-climate plants.
Open: daily during daylight hours.

Mount Wilson Gardens
The Mount Wilson area, also along the Bell's Line of Road, contains many private gardens which are open to the public during the spring and autumn months. Check with the local tourist authority while in the mountains.

CANBERRA
The Australian National Botanic Gardens
These lovely gardens contain a large collection of unusual Australian native plants (see page 110).
Clunies Ross Street, Black Mountain. Open: daily 9am–5pm.

CENTRAL COAST
Askania Park, Gosford
This 41-hectare garden features rainforest: of both the sub-tropical and warm temperate varieties. A short walk takes you past over 100 different specimens of such plants.
Ourimbah Creek Road, near Gosford. Open: Wednesday to Sunday 9am–5pm. Access by car from Ourimbah.

Picnics with a view!

*P*icnics and barbecues are a way of life in Australia, and there is no better place for dining *al fresco* than overlooking the world's finest harbour. Sydney Harbour has many popular and lesser-known grassy lookouts and headlands which provide wonderful views while you eat outdoors: these are some of the best.

Balls Head Reserve, Waverton
This little-known, quiet spot has barbecue facilities and picnic tables and overlooks the inner harbour – from here there are excellent views of the western side of the Harbour Bridge.
Train to Waverton Station and then walk.

Taking a breather in the Domain

Balmoral Beach, Mosman
This popular northside beach is divided into two by Rocky Point – an ideal setting for a picnic. From the grass here there are fine views of Middle Harbour and North Head, and the nearby beach is excellent for a swim.
Ferry to Taronga Zoo, then bus 238.

Cremorne Point Reserve
Another delightful northside spot is

Cremorne Point, which is a short ferry ride from Circular Quay. From the wharf turn left and walk into the reserve: a few metres along the grassy bank there is a small swimming pool. Another perfect picnic spot!
Ferry from Circular Quay.

McKell Park, Darling Point
Located in the up-market suburb of Darling Point, this small, well-manicured park is one of the city's prettiest. There are two levels of gardens, created around the foundations of an old mansion, and the park even has its own private jetty which juts out into the harbour opposite Clark Island. This hidden corner of the city is known only to Darling Point locals and is rarely overcrowded.
At the end of Darling Point Road. Open: during daylight hours (the park has toilets). Bus 327 from Circular Quay.

Mrs Macquarie's Point, The Domain
A much more popular picnic and harbour-viewing area, but during weekdays you can always find a quiet spot away from the busloads of visitors who usually stay only briefly. From the point there are marvellous close-up views of the Opera House and Sydney Harbour Bridge, and a fine outlook across to the north shore.
Free bus number 666 to the Art Gallery,

then walk (nearest toilets in the Botanic Gardens).

Nielsen Park, Vaucluse
The beach and park here get very crowded at weekends, but walk up on to the cliff on the right-hand side of the beach, and it's possible to find a quieter spot. This is part of the Sydney Harbour National Park and there are excellent views of the harbour. Nielsen Park has toilet facilities, as well as a food and drink kiosk.
Bus 325 from Circular Quay.

North Head, Manly
There are more wonderful views from this point overlooking South Head and the harbour, and it's rarely crowded. See pages 34–5 for more details.
Jetcat or ferry from Circular Quay.

South Head, Watsons Bay
This smaller promontory is across the

A place to pause with a glorious view

water from North Head and is capped by a lighthouse. There is a beach, and toilet facilities at nearby Camp Cove. See pages 32–3 for further information.
Bus 324 or 325 (or ferry on weekends) from Circular Quay.

Sydney Harbour Islands
Harbour islands such as Clark (opposite Darling Point) and Shark (out in Rose Bay) may be booked in advance for the day from the National Parks and Wildlife Service. Visitors are almost guaranteed privacy, but the catch is that they must provide their own transport. It's easy, however, to hire a water taxi. For further details, call National Parks on 585 6333.

Other good spots on the north side that are best reached by car are Dobroyd Head, Balgowlah and Bradleys Head, Mosman.

Wildlife

Native birds are often br
with co

The kangaroo has become a
symbol of Australia

The delightf
koa

The colourful plumage
of the rainbow lorikeet

Australia's extraordinary wildlife is fascinating and unique: it has evolved over millions of years in total isolation from the rest of the world.

The continent's favourite mammals are found nowhere else in the world: these marsupial, or pouched, creatures give birth to 'premature' young who complete their development in the mother's pouch. The popular Australian symbol, the kangaroo, is a marsupial, as are the wallaby, quokka, wombat, echidna (spiny ant-eater), certain mice and a wide variety of possums. The universal favourite, though, must be the cute, cuddly koala. This endangered creature is undoubtedly one of Australia's most important tourist assets.

The rarely seen nocturnal platypus, along with the echidna, are the world's only monotremes – egg-laying mammals. But unlike the latter, the shy, river-dwelling platypus does not have a pouch.

Some of the wildlife is not so cuddly.

Australia has more than 140 species of snakes, of which about 100 are venomous. Among the most dangerous of these are the taipan, tiger snake, brown snake, copperhead and death adder, all of which should be avoided, or at least treated with the greatest respect! There are also plenty of harmless lizards, including the large, cheeky goanna: don't be surprised if one invades your campsite to lick out the frying pan!

The bird life is extraordinary too. From the large, flightless emu, which can run at a speed of 48kph, to the tiny fig parrot and the ever-noisy kookaburra, the continent is a birdwatcher's paradise. The most spectacular birds are the many brilliantly coloured parrots such as the multi-hued lorikeets, budgerigars and pretty rosellas.

Most of this wonderful wildlife can be seen in New South Wales, and even around the Sydney region. The state's numerous national parks are the best bet, or visit one of the many wildlife sanctuaries for a close-up encounter.

Kookaburra - its loud, laughing call is one of the country's best-known sounds

Shopping

*S*hopping in Sydney's pleasant environment is an enjoyable experience and there is a great deal for the visitor to choose from, especially in the burgeoning area of 'Australiana'. Recent years have seen the inevitable array of tacky souvenirs thankfully swamped by Australian-designed and produced goods of extremely high quality, which any visitor would be proud to take home.

A welcoming sign at The Rocks

Beach, surfing and resort wear are excellent buys. The designs and styles of swimwear, T-shirts, sweatshirts and shorts are innovative and colourful, and design houses such as Mambo, Done Art and Design and Weiss Art have turned such clothing into a virtual art form. The latter two companies run their own shops in the city and Rocks areas and also sell a variety of attractive souvenirs. Other Australian souvenirs, particularly those with an Aboriginal emphasis, are extremely popular. Names to look for include Viva

La Wombat, and Desert Designs.

Traditional Australian clothing, such as Akubra hats, moleskin trousers, riding boots and Drizabone oilskin coats are great buys. Head for outfitters such as R M Williams (389 George Street) and Morrisons (105 George Street, The Rocks).

Opals are one of the world's most colourful precious stones and the Australian varieties are particularly prized. There are many opal shops in The Rocks, Darling Harbour and the city centre. A bonus is that the stones are tax-free for visitors.

Sheep and kangaroo skins in the form of rugs, toys, coats and slippers are another popular, and inexpensive, Australian product. Furry souvenirs of a different variety come as toy kangaroos, wombats, koalas and other marsupials of all sizes. Most tourist stores stock these, but there are some excellent shops in The Rocks.

Other unique purchases include **Australian foodstuffs** (macadamia nuts, for example) and wines, **Aboriginal art and artefacts**, Australian art, crafts, hand-knitted sweaters and books. Visitors should also remember that duty- and tax-free prices in Australia are very competitive and there are many duty-free stores in the city centre, as well as at the airport.

The best city shopping is found at The Rocks, Darling Harbour and the central Pitt, George and Castlereagh Streets area, while the many markets, and suburbs such as Paddington and Double Bay, offer some unusual and innovative purchases.

THE ROCKS

Not only is The Rocks area Sydney's sightseeing magnet, it also offers some of the most interesting city shopping.

George Street

Plenty of shopping here! A walk along this street will provide most visitors with all their souvenir needs.

Done Art and Design at 123-125 George Street offers colourful, naive-design beach wear, T-shirts, sweatshirts, homewares and other high-quality souvenirs. Behind the main shop is the **Art Director's Gallery** at 21 Nurses Walk, which sells prints and other work by the internationally-renowned artist, Ken Done. As a contrast, the nearby **Weiss Art** collection comes in stark but attractive black and white designs, featuring Australian animals. Beach and leisure wear, as well as homewares, are available.

Opal Fields (155 George Street) and **Flame Opals** (119 George Street) are the best Rocks locations for these popular gemstones.

Morrisons at 105 George Street offers Aussie bush wear: Akubra hats, riding boots and other uniquely Australian products. They also sell wonderful hand-knits and other Australian- designed clothing.

The Earth Exchange museum, just off George Street on Hickson Road, includes a shop selling opals and other gems, while at 117 George Street there is

A typical design by Ken Done

an excellent Aboriginal gallery and shop. *Tel: 251 2422.*

The Crafts Council Gallery (100 George Street) is not cheap, but here you will find some of Australia's finest contemporary weaving, pottery, jewellery and other crafts. Another good Rocks craft centre is **Australian Craftworks** at 127 George Street.

Argyle Street

Branching off George Street, this road also offers some good shopping opportunities. The **Aussie Bear** shop, opposite the Argyle Centre, stocks excellent Australian-theme soft toys. The **Argyle Centre** itself is an old warehouse complex which sells sheepskin products, crafts, books, stationery, T-shirts, jewellery and leather goods. Opposite, **Clocktower Square** at the corner of Argyle and Harrington Streets contains shops selling souvenirs, leisure and resort wear and many other items.

City Centre

The best central city shopping area is on George, Pitt and Castlereagh Streets, between Park and King Streets.

GEORGE STREET
Dymocks
This is one of Sydney's best and largest book and stationery shops, with a comprehensive Australiana section. *Between Market and King Streets.*

The luxurious world of David Jones

Queen Victoria Building
The vast QVB was built in 1898 and is now Sydney's most historic and attractive shopping centre, featuring leadlight glass windows and beautiful tiled floors. The four levels contain cafés and restaurants, and everything from exclusive fashion designer outlets to duty-free shops and numerous opal, craft and souvenir stores. *Between Druitt and Market Streets.*

PITT STREET MALL
This pedestrian mall, between Market and King Streets, is the main shopping precinct and includes the Grace Bros department store, Virgin Records, several arcades (including the Mid City Centre) and many chain stores.

Angus & Robertson
This bookshop has a large collection of material on Australia – including plenty of guidebooks, maps and travelogues.

Centrepoint and the Imperial Arcade
These two connecting arcades contain a vast number of shops, selling everything from handbags to newspapers. Many of the most popular chain and clothing stores are located here.

Strand Arcade
Running between Pitt and George Streets, the Strand is another attractive old-style shopping arcade. The three levels of shops here include clothing, jewellery and souvenir outlets, but visitors will also enjoy the Strand's historic ambience.

CASTLEREAGH STREET
David Jones'
In the block behind Pitt Street Mall lies Sydney's largest and best department store, which has been called 'the most beautiful store in the world'. The Elizabeth Street building dates from 1927, but 1980s renovations have created a world of glass, mirrors and marble that is a pleasure to shop in. The Castlereagh store, just across the road, has an excellent food and wine department in the basement – Sydney's modest answer to Harrods' food hall.

Corner of Elizabeth, Castlereagh and Market Streets.

Skygarden
This luxurious, modern centre runs between Castlereagh and Pitt Streets and offers some excellent shopping in very pleasant surroundings.

MLC Centre
Further towards Martin Place, the MLC Centre is another shopping precinct, which includes some of the city's most up-market shops.

DARLING HARBOUR AREA
This precinct, on the western side of the city, offers not only museums and parks, but a large shopping and eating area.

Harbourside
The complex contains around 200 shops, including Done Art and Design, Weiss Art, craft shops and the usual chain stores. The shops here are open from 10am to 9pm Monday to Saturday, and to 6pm on Sundays. There are also 50 food stalls and a number of waterfront restaurants.

Chinatown
This is just behind the southern part of George Street, and near the Darling Harbour complex. Chinatown is an interesting area, particularly for its food shops. There are also some bargains to be found among the racks of genuine Chinese T-shirts, canvas shoes and homewares.
Haymarket.

OTHER CITY SHOPS
There is a variety of interesting shopping venues just outside the city centre.

The Strand Arcade in Sydney

Art Gallery of New South Wales
The AGNSW shop sells an excellent range of posters, prints and cards featuring the works of Australian, and other, artists and has a comprehensive book selection.
Art Gallery Road, the Domain.

Australian Museum
The museum shop is excellent for books, cards and unusual souvenirs with an Australian theme. The museum is located just across the park from David Jones' department store.
College Street.

Markets

Sydney's many markets offer the visitor the ideal opportunity to join (and observe!) the locals in their shopping pursuits. The city's markets are colourful and fun, and you are likely to pick up a bargain or two. Most are located on the city fringes, or in some of the more interesting suburbs. In addition to those detailed here, weekend markets are also held at Kirribilli and Manly.

ANTIQUE MARKETS

The inner east suburbs of Paddington, Woollahra and Surry Hills are home to many antique shops and markets for the browser and buyer. Two large indoor markets are: the **Sydney Antique Centre** (531 South Dowling Street, Surry Hills), which is open daily from 10.30am to 6pm; and the **Woollahra Galleries** at 160 Oxford Street, Woollahra.

Balmain Market

This market is held in one of the inner city's most fascinating areas – a visit will give you an excuse to wander the picturesque streets of this old harbourside suburb. Items on sale include arts and crafts, clothing and antiques.
St Andrews Church, Darling Street, Balmain. Open: Saturday 7.30am–4pm.

Paddington Bazaar

This is another Saturday market, and the most colourful, popular and interesting that the city has to offer. In addition to the large number of stalls selling weird and wonderful clothing, jewellery, crafts, books, second-hand items and foodstuffs, the clientele are a major attraction. Shoppers include anyone from yuppies to black-clad punks and ageing hippies. There's also a wholefood café inside the church hall, and buskers

play outside. Children enjoy the atmosphere too.
Village Church, Oxford Street, Paddington. Open: Saturday 10am–5pm.

Paddy's Markets

This Sydney institution, located next to Redfern Railway Station, is a vast indoor market on a permanent site, just one train stop from Central Station. In addition to clothing, handicrafts and tourist items, it is a fruit, vegetable and produce market where locals go to buy their essentials at bargain prices – particularly at the end of the day.
Open: Saturday and Sunday 8am–6pm.

The Rocks Market

Held in upper George Street, this 100-stall market specialises in antiques, crafts, homewares and decorative items.
Open: Saturday and Sunday 10am–6pm.

SUBURBAN SHOPPING

For those who prefer to shop away from the busy streets of the Central Business District, there are many suburban shopping centres within easy train or bus access from the city centre. These vary from modern shopping malls to groups of more exclusive, individual shops.

Balmain

Balmain's main thoroughfare, Darling

Street, is packed with interesting, 'alternative' bookshops, craft shops, delicatessens and boutiques.

Double Bay

This inner east harbourside area (nicknamed Double Pay) is where you'll find the most exclusive Australian, French and Italian designer clothes, shoes and accessory shops. Even if you cannot afford to shop here, it's a very pleasant suburb to wander around.

Paddington

Paddington's Oxford Street, from Victoria Barracks to Jersey Road, is great for bookshops, records, unusual clothes and interesting pieces of Australiana. An excellent street for shopping, browsing and general café life.

Shopping Malls

Large modern shopping malls, which contain department and chain stores, are located at Bondi Junction, in the eastern suburbs, and Chatswood, on the north shore.

COUNTRY SHOPPING

NSW country towns offer similar shopping facilities to those in Sydney suburbs, but there are more individual buys in certain areas.

Blue Mountains

The picturesque mountain towns of Katoomba, Leura and Mount Victoria contain a range of antique and craft shops which will be of interest to the visitor.

Inland

In rural centres like Armidale, Tamworth, Orange or Albury, look out for traditional Australian clothing such as Akubra hats and Drizabone raincoats.

The Blackwater Bay Fish Market

Outback

Opals can be bought straight from the source in the outback settlements of Lightning Ridge and White Cliffs.

Southern Highlands

The towns here, particularly Berrima and Moss Vale, have many craft and antiques shops and also specialise in home-made produce such as fudge, sweetmeats and jams.

Wine Areas

Wine is the obvious purchase in the vineyard regions of Mudgee and the Hunter Valley.

Entertainment

*T*he Sydney entertainment scene offers something for everyone – be it opera, classical music, jazz, a rock concert, nightclubbing, the thriving gay scene or the movies. There is also a great deal on offer to keep the children entertained. The visitor will be spoiled for choice, especially if on a short visit.

Home of Sydney's classical entertainment

What's on?

The *Sydney Morning Herald* publishes the comprehensive blue-coloured *Metro* guide on Fridays. This 20-page supplement lists every imaginable form of entertainment for the coming week. If you miss this, the *Saturday Herald* also has a detailed entertainment section. Another useful publication is *On the Street*, a free weekly newspaper, available at pubs and clubs, which covers the rock music scene.

Tickets

Sydney's central ticket agency, Ticketek, offers a simple alternative to buying tickets directly from the various venues,

and there is also an excellent half-price ticket system – see the **Practical Guide** for details. Tickets for cinemas and musical performances at the smaller venues must be bought from the relevant establishment.

Prices

Tickets for the opera and ballet tend to be expensive, but other entertainment is usually reasonably priced.

CLASSICAL ENTERTAINMENT

Sydney's days of being somewhat erroneously regarded as a cultural backwater are long over. The city offers a sophisticated scene for lovers of classical music, opera, ballet and theatre at many venues.

The home of classical entertainment in Sydney is undoubtedly the Sydney Opera House. The complex includes the opera theatre, a concert hall, and a drama theatre and playhouse, which stage a wide variety of productions by the Australian Opera, Australian Ballet, Sydney Symphony Orchestra, Sydney Theatre Company and Sydney Philharmonia Choir. Events also feature performances by visiting world-class international companies and orchestras. *For information on any performance at the Opera House, telephone the box office on 250 7777.*

In country areas, where even the largest towns have a relatively small population, there is little in the way of classical entertainment. The cities of Newcastle and Wollongong, and some large country towns such as Orange, for example, have better than average theatre facilities and host Sydney productions from time to time. If you are travelling around NSW and something special is on in town, you'll be sure to hear about it!

BALLET AND OPERA

The Australian Ballet and Australian Opera companies perform regularly at the Opera House. For more information on performances you can either call the Opera House, or the two companies direct:

Australian Ballet. Tel: 699 8499.
Australian Opera. Tel: 319 1088.

SYMPHONY CONCERTS

Although the Sydney Opera House is the home of the city's classical music scene, concerts are often performed at Sydney Town Hall, on George Street. In addition, the NSW State Conservatorium of Music in the Domain holds concerts given by its students. *Tel: 230 1263* for information.

The Sydney Opera House Trust offers free summer lunchtime concerts on Wednesdays – they are held at a variety of venues around the Opera House.

Sydney Symphony Orchestra

This excellent company performs around 90 concerts each year and often features distinguished overseas musicians in addition to local talent.
More information can be obtained by calling 552 0552.

THEATRE

Sydney has over 20 theatre venues which stage anything from Shakespeare to Simon and Sondheim. The major theatres tend to stick to international mainstream and musical productions, while many small venues around the city present innovative and experimental theatre. Check the *Metro* guide for details.

Sydney Theatre Company

The city's leading theatre company offers excellent drama both by the classical playwrights, and by leading Australian writers such as David Williamson. Famous actors like Bryan Brown and Britain's Warren Mitchell often perform for the company.
Telephone 250 1700 for more information.

MAJOR THEATRES

Her Majesty's Theatre
107 Quay Street, City. Tel: 212 3411.
Seymour Theatre Centre
Corner City Road and Cleveland Street, Chippendale. Tel: 692 3511.
Sydney Opera House Drama Theatre
Sydney Opera House, City. Tel: 250 7777.
Theatre Royal MLC Centre
King Street, City. Tel: 231 6111.
Wharf Theatre Pier 4
Hickson Road, Millers Point.
Tel: 250 1777.

OTHER THEATRES

Belvoir Street Theatre
25 Belvoir Street, Surry Hills.
Tel: 699 3444. (Eastern suburbs)
Ensemble Theatre
78 McDougall Street, Milson's Point.
Tel: 929 0644. (North Shore)
Marian Street Theatre
2 Marian Street, Killara.
Tel: 498 3166. (North Shore.)

Music, Dance and Shows

*A*lthough Sydney offers much for the more 'cultural' tastes in entertainment, the city is also well-prepared for those who want to let off steam in a nightclub, or enjoy a night of cabaret, modern music or dance performances – all tastes are catered for.

Jazz in the open air

CABARET AND THEATRE RESTAURANTS

These popular establishments provide entertainment with dinner.

The Comedy Store. Comedy with or without dinner, at very reasonable prices.
278 Cleveland Street, Surry Hills.
Tel: 319 5731.
Kinselas. Cabaret and comedy shows in a stylish, renovated funeral parlour!
383 Bourke Street, Taylor Square.
Tel: 331 6200.
Tilbury Hotel. An unpretentious inner-city pub that hosts some of Sydney's best cabaret.
Corner of Forbes and Nicholson Streets,
Woolloomooloo. Tel: 357 1914.

DANCE

The internationally acclaimed **Sydney Dance Company** *(tel: 221 4811)* is the city's premier modern dance ensemble. Their innovative performances take place at the Opera House and a number of other venues. Look out also for the **Aboriginal Islander Dance Theatre.** Phone *660 2851* for details.

MODERN MUSIC

The city's main venues for rock and popular music concerts are the vast **Sydney Entertainment Centre** at Darling Harbour *(tel: 1 1582)*, and the wonderful, more intimate, art-deco

State Theatre in the heart of the city at 49 Market Street *(tel: 264 2431)*. The Enmore Theatre *(tel: 550 3666)* in the inner west also stages rock concerts from time to time. Refer to entertainment guides, or call Ticketek, to find out what's on while you are in town.

FOLK

This isn't big in Sydney, but there are several pubs which cater for the folk music audience. Check the *Metro* guide for details.

JAZZ AND BLUES

Sydney has more than enough jazz and blues music to please any fan. The venues are many, but the following are some of the best.

Don Burrows Supper Club

Sophisticated surroundings in Sydney's best hotel. Jazz from Tuesday to Saturday.
The Regent of Sydney, 199 George Street, City. Tel: 238 0000.

Harbourside Brasserie

Jazz and blues in a harbourside setting.
Pier One, Dawes Point. Tel: 252 3000.

Real Ale Café & Tavern

Food, a selection of over 80 beers, and good jazz from Wednesday to Friday.
66 King Street, City. Tel: 262 3277.

Round Midnight

An excellent nightclub specialising in live jazz and blues. Open nightly from 8pm to 3am.
2 Roslyn Street, Kings Cross. Tel: 356 4045.

Soup Plus Restaurant

Jazz and cheap food in this great basement atmosphere.
383 George Street, City. Tel: 299 7728. Open: Monday to Saturday.

PUB AND CLUB ROCK

Sydney is full of pubs and clubs which host live rock music provided by innumerable bands, on most nights of the week. Check the *Metro* guide, but the following are some of the more popular venues.

CITY

The Craig Brewery Bar & Grill
Darling Harbour. Tel: 281 3922.
Pumphouse Tavern Brewery
17 Little Pier Street, Darling Harbour. Tel: 299 1841.

EASTERN SUBURBS

Cock 'N' Bull Tavern
89 Ebley Street, Bondi Junction. Tel: 389 3004.
Coogee Bay Hotel
253 Coogee Bay Road, Coogee. Tel: 665 0000.
Paddington–Woollahra RSL Club
226 Oxford Street, Paddington. Tel: 331 1203.
Springfield Bar & Grill
15 Springfield Avenue, Kings Cross. Tel: 358 1785.

INNER WEST

Annandale Hotel
17 Parramatta Road, Annandale. Tel: 550 1078.
Birkenhead Point Tavern
Birkenhead Point, Drummoyne. Tel: 81 4238.

NORTH SHORE

North Sydney Leagues Club
20 Abbott Street, Cammeray. Tel: 955 6101.

Nightclubs and Discos

Most of Sydney's nightclubs and discotheques are to be found in the city centre, and around the Kings Cross and Darlinghurst areas of the inner east. There is plenty of choice for all age groups and tastes. Clubs generally stay open to around 3am and most establishments don't really get going until midnight. Cover charges and drinks prices vary considerably, with clubs around Oxford Street, for example, charging far less than somewhere more sophisticated like Juliana's at the Hilton Hotel. The following are some of the more popular establishments.

The Cauldron Open nightly. Dance and dine with a super-trendy crowd.
207 Darlinghurst Road, Darlinghurst.
Tel: 331 1523.

The Freezer Popular with a younger, trendy age group. Open Wednesday to Saturday.
11 Oxford Street, Paddington.
Tel: 332 2568.

Jackson's on George Funky live and disco music. Open Tuesday to Saturday.
176 George Street, City. Tel: 247 2727.

Juliana's Open from Tuesday to Saturday. Glossy and expensive; for the older age group.
Sydney Hilton Hotel, 259 Pitt Street, City.
Tel: 266 0610.

Metropolis Open Monday to Saturday. An elegant nightclub, restaurant and cocktail piano bar.
99 Walker Street, North Sydney.
Tel: 954 3599.

Rogues Another trendy inner-city nightclub. Open until the small hours.
10 Oxford Square, Darlinghurst.
Tel: 332 1718.

Site Night Club Popular with a younger, black-clad set.
171 Victoria Street, Potts Point.
Tel: 358 6511.

Studebaker's Bar Open daily except Monday; features mostly '50s and '60s

A sign to please the energetic

rock-and-roll in an American-style setting.
33 Bayswater Road, Kings Cross.
Tel: 358 5656.

Williams An upmarket hotel nightclub.
Boulevard Hotel, 90 William Street, City.
Tel: 357 2277.

OTHER ENTERTAINMENT
CINEMA

Sydney's major cinemas are located south of Town Hall on George Street (between Bathurst and Liverpool Streets), and on Pitt Street, between Market and Park Streets. **Hoyts** (505 George Street) and the **Greater Union** cinemas at George City (525 George Street) and the Pitt Centre (232 Pitt Street) are multi-cinema complexes which screen mass appeal films, as does The **Village Cinema City** at 545 George Street.

Alternative and 'art' films are shown at the Academy Twin (3a Oxford Street) and the Australian Film Institute (Paddington Town Hall, corner of Oxford Street and Oatley Road) cinemas in Paddington; the Valhalla in Glebe (166 Glebe Point Road); the Dendy (MLC Centre, Martin Place, City); and the Walker in North Sydney (121 Walker Street).

There are cinemas in most of the larger suburbs, but some of the more central are located at Bondi Junction, Cremorne, Double Bay, Mosman, Randwick and Stanmore.

Studebaker's bar re-creates the '50s

GAMBLING

Unlike most of Australia, NSW has no casinos, which is an undoubted frustration for the state's many keen punters. The alternative is to put a bet on the horses, dogs or football through the TAB (Totalizator Agency Board) which has many outlets throughout the city, or play the infamous 'pokies'. These poker machines are a ubiquitous and noisy fixture in most clubs, but are an extremely popular form of entertainment. If you are interested, visit any of the local RSL (Returned Servicemen's League) or Leagues (Rugby League) Clubs around Sydney or in country towns. Another option is the Aussie Rules Club at 28 Darlinghurst Road, Kings Cross.

THE GAY SCENE

The gay scene is flourishing in Sydney, particularly in Darlinghurst's Oxford Street, known locally as 'The Great Gay Way'. The stretch between Hyde Park and Glenmore Road is full of pubs and clubs, such as The Albury at 6 Oxford Street, Paddington, and the Midnight Shift (85 Oxford Street, Darlinghurst), which cater for a mostly male gay clientele.

NIGHT TOURS

Tours of the city at night, taking in dinner and a visit to a club or show, are operated by tour companies such as AAT King's *(tel: 252 2788)* and Australian Pacific Tours *(tel: 252 2988)*.

OUTDOOR ENTERTAINMENT

This is something that Sydney specialises in. Outdoor entertainment suits the climate and general carefree atmosphere, and virtually all of it is free.

The best spots are the Martin Place amphitheatre on weekday lunchtimes, and Sundays at the Opera House, The Rocks and Darling Harbour. Entertainment can be anything from jazz bands to jugglers, ethnic music to Morris dancers. Circular Quay is a good spot to be entertained by buskers of every description while waiting for a ferry. You could also visit Sydney's version of Speakers' Corner

Children

*S*ydney is a city for the young, and especially the young at heart. However, once the major sights have been seen, there is much that will be particularly entertaining for the children. There are museums, wildlife parks and aquariums, theme parks, outdoor activities, and even a children's theatre, to sample.

MUSEUMS

The following museums are particularly interesting for children.

Australian Museum

Excellent natural history and Aboriginal displays.
6 College Street, City. Tel: 339 8111. Open: daily 10am–5pm (admission fee). Train to Museum Station.

Museum of Australian Childhood

19th-and 20th-century children's toys, books and illustrations.
Juniper Hall, 250 Oxford Street, Paddington. Tel: 332 1988. Open: Tuesday to Sunday 10am–4pm (admission fee). Bus 380 from Circular Quay.

Powerhouse Museum

Science, technology and social history, with lots of 'hands-on' participation for children.
500 Harris Street, Ultimo. Tel: 217 0100. Open: daily 10am–5pm (admission fee: special family tickets). Monorail to The Haymarket

The Story of Sydney

A combination of cinema, theatre and exhibitions relating Sydney's history.
100 George Street, The Rocks. Tel: 247 7777. Open: daily 10am–5pm (admission fee: special family tickets). Bus or train to Circular Quay.

OUTDOOR ACTIVITIES
Bounty Cruises

For a special treat, cruise the Harbour on the replica of the famous *Bounty*.
Tel: 247 1789. Daily cruises.

Royal Botanic Gardens

A wonderful spot for a stroll or picnic. Free guided walks operate from the Visitor Centre at 10am on Wednesdays and Fridays, and at 1pm on Sundays.
Tel: 231 8111. Open: daily 6.30am–sunset (free admission). Sydney Explorer Bus or free bus 666 to the Art Gallery.

OUTDOOR ENTERTAINMENT
Darling Harbour

In addition to the Sydney Aquarium, Powerhouse Museum and National Maritime Museum, the complex provides free musical entertainment, eating, shopping and a funfair.
Tel: 0055 20261 for entertainment information. Monorail from Pitt Street, or ferry from Circular Quay.

The Rocks

Free entertainment is provided in The Rocks Square from 11am to 3pm on Sundays.
Tel: 11606 for entertainment information.

Sydney Opera House

On Sunday afternoons, free outdoor entertainment is provided around the

Opera House. The usual offerings are market stalls, buskers, jazz bands and strolling musicians.
Tel: 250 7250 for entertainment information.

THEATRE
Marian Street Children's Theatre
Varying theatrical productions.
2 Marian Street, Killara. Tel: 498 3166. Train to Killara from Town Hall (North Shore line).

THEME PARKS
The following charge an admission fee.

Australiana Pioneer Village
A re-creation of a 19th-century pioneer village.
Buttsworth Lane, Wilberforce. Tel: (045) 75 1457. Open: Wednesday to Sunday 10am–5pm. Train to Windsor.

Australia's Wonderland
Australia's largest theme park with a wide range of shows and attractions.
Wallgrove Road, Minchinbury. Tel: 675 0100. Open: weekends (and school and public holidays) from late September to mid-July, 10am–5pm. Train to Rooty Hill and then a shuttle bus.

Old Sydney Town
Experience life in Sydney as it was 200 years ago!
Pacific Highway, Somersby, Central Coast. Tel: (043) 40 1104. Open: Wednesday to Sunday 10am –5pm (also school and public holidays). Train to Gosford, then coach.

WILDLIFE
All of the following charge for admission.

Koala Park Sanctuary
Sydney's best-known koala sanctuary.
Castle Hill Road, West Pennant Hills.

The entrance to Taronga Zoo

Tel: 484 3141. Open: daily 9am–5pm. Train to Pennant Hills and bus 655.

Manly Oceanarium
This underwater aquarium is built on the bottom of the sea. View fish, sharks, stingrays and seals from a moving footway inside a transparent tunnel.
West Esplanade, Manly. Tel: 949 2644. Open: daily 10am–5pm. Ferry or Jetcat from Circular Quay.

Sydney Aquarium
Fun for all the family: features the fish and marine life of Australia.
Darling Harbour. Tel: 262 2300. Open: daily 9.30am–9pm. Monorail from Pitt Street or ferry from Circular Quay.

Taronga Zoo
There are fine harbour and city views as well as a good collection of animals.
Bradleys Head Road, Mosman. Tel: 969 2777. Open: daily 9am–5pm. Ferry from Circular Quay.

Waratah Park
Australian birds and animals in a lovely native bushland setting.
Namba Road, Duffy's Forest. Tel: 450 2377. Open: daily 10am–5pm. Train to Chatswood, then Forest Coach Lines bus 56.

Sport

*G*ood weather, relatively unpolluted air and the abundance of waterways and open spaces make Sydney and New South Wales a sporting paradise. It is easy to arrange a game of tennis, a round of golf, sailing, surfing or a horse ride at one of the state's many venues. For those not interested in participating, there is a host of exciting spectator sports at numerous locations throughout Sydney – everything from tennis to rugby league, or sailing to horse racing.

WATERSPORTS
Sydney's 60km of coastline and the vast waterways of Port Jackson, Pittwater, Broken Bay, the Hawkesbury and Georges Rivers and Port Hacking create amazing opportunities for watersports. The long NSW coastline, as well as the state's many inland rivers and waterways, also provide some great watersport locations.

CANOEING AND KAYAKING
Sea kayaking can be practised virtually anywhere along the NSW coast, but there are also many inland waterways for canoeing enthusiasts. Some of the best venues are the placid Myall Lakes region and the Shoalhaven River, to the south

of the city. In the Sydney region, canoes and kayaks can be hired from:

Bush and Paddle Sports, Sylvania. *Tel: 544.7628.*
Q Craft Canoes and Kayaks, Manly Vale. *Tel: 907 9766.*

SAILBOARDING (WINDSURFING)
The best city sailboarding spots are on Sydney Harbour, Pittwater, or at Narrabeen Lakes to the north of Manly. Equipment is available for hire:

Balmoral Sailboard Centre and School, The Spit. *Tel: 969 4002.*
Klaus Windsurfing and Sailing School, Narrabeen. *Tel: 913 1765.*
Northside Sailing School, The Spit. *Tel: 969 3972.*
Rose Bay Windsurfer School. *Tel: 371 7036.*

SAILING
Yachting enthusiasts can book a sail through one of the many sailing schools. It is also possible to hire a boat for the day.

Australian Sailing School and Club, Mosman. *Tel: 960 3077.*

A young surfer takes to the waves

Eastsail, Rushcutters Bay. *Tel: 327 1166.*
Pacific Sailing School, Rushcutters Bay. *Tel: 326 2399.*

SCUBA DIVING

Although the Sydney area provides adequate scuba diving spots that offer some interesting wreck diving, the best venues are at Lord Howe Island, Byron Bay and Coffs Harbour to the north, and Jervis Bay, south of Sydney. Several Sydney operators arrange such diving holidays:

Deep 6 Diving, Manly. *Tel: 977 5966.*
Dive 2000, Neutral Bay. *Tel: 953 7783.*
Pro-Diving Services, Coogee. *Tel: 665 6333.*

SURFING

This quintessential Australian sport began at Manly beach in the 1890s, and today it is as popular with Australian kids as skateboarding is in most other countries. If you want to have a go, or are already an experienced surfer, there are many excellent beaches in Sydney and along the NSW coast. See pages 42–3 for more details of surfing beaches.

SWIMMING

Sydney has swimming venues to suit all tastes – from surf-fringed ocean beaches to placid harbour bays, or, if you prefer, public pools.

Harbour beaches

See pages 42–3, but good choices are Nielsen Park, Parsley Bay and Camp Cove on the south shore, and Balmoral north of the harbour.

Ocean surf beaches

From north to south, recommended

The Olympic Pool's unrivalled setting

sandy ocean beaches are: Palm Beach, Whale Beach, Avalon, Newport, Collaroy, Manly, Bondi, Bronte, Coogee, Maroubra and Cronulla.

Swimming pools

There are many public pools in Sydney: the 'Boy' Charlton and North Sydney pools have attractive harbourside locations. Admission charges are minimal.

Andrew 'Boy' Charlton Pool, The Domain. *Tel: 358 6686.*
Dawn Fraser Pool, Balmain. *Tel: 810 2183.*
North Sydney Olympic Pool, Milson's Point. *Tel: 955 2309.*
Prince Alfred Park Swimming Pool, Surry Hills. *Tel: 319 7045.*

NSW Beaches

The entire NSW coastline has hundreds of wonderful, sandy and often uncrowded beaches. Some particularly good beach areas are (from north to south): Byron Bay/Ballina, the region north of Coffs Harbour, the Port Stephens area, Jervis Bay and Merimbula/Eden in the far south.

Participant Sports

The state's wonderful climate means that sport can be enjoyed all year round, although the summer heat often drives locals to the water, rather than the tennis court! For adventure activities such as bushwalking, cycling and rock sports, see also Organised Tours in the **Practical Guide**.

BUSHWALKING
Opportunities abound, both in the Sydney region and further afield. Routes can be anything from an easy coastal walk from the Spit Bridge to Manly on Sydney's north shore, to a two-day Royal National Park hike.
For information on walking in national parks, contact the National Parks and Wildlife Service. Tel: 585 6333.

CYCLING
The best Sydney city venue is at Centennial Park, where bicycles are available for hire for a small fee.

Centennial Park Cycles, Randwick. *Tel: 398 5027.*

A round of golf at Pittwater

GOLF
Unlike many countries, where golf is only for the rich and influential, in Australia the sport is relatively cheap, and golf courses are plentiful. There are some 375 in NSW, and around 80 in the Sydney region. The following courses are open to all, but you should phone to book a game:

Sydney
Bondi Golf Club, North Bondi. *Tel: 30 1981.*
Lane Cove River Golf Course. *Tel: 428 1316.*
Moore Park Golf Club. *Tel: 663 3791.*
Woollahra Golf Club, Rose Bay. *Tel: 327 5404.*

The following are some of the state's best golf courses:
Blue Mountains
Leura Golf Club. *Tel: (047) 82 5011.*
Canberra
Yowani Country Club. *Tel: (06) 241 3377.*
Central Coast
Gosford Golf Club. *Tel: (043) 25 0361.*
Murray River
Albury Golf Club. *Tel: (060) 21 3411.*
North Coast
Grafton Golf Club. *Tel: (066) 43 1595.*
Snowy Mountains
Cooma Golf Club. *Tel: (064) 52 2243.*
South Coast

Pambula–Merimbula Golf Club.
Tel: (064) 95 6154.

GYMNASIUMS

If you are interested in working out,
there are plenty of options in this fitness-
crazy city. The most central gym is:

City Gym, East Sydney. _Tel: 360 6247._

HORSE RIDING

Within inner Sydney, the most popular
horse riding location is Centennial Park,
where horses can be hired for a ride.
Otford, near the Royal National Park, is
another suggestion.

Blue Ribbon Riding School, Moore
Park. _Tel: 361 3859._
Centennial Park Horse Hire, Moore
Park. _Tel: 332 2770._
Otford Valley Farm, Otford. _Tel: (042)
94 2442._

JOGGING/RUNNING

Sydney is jogging mad and there are
many jogging/fitness tracks to work out
on. There are also plenty of scenic open
spaces such as Bondi Beach, Manly
Beach, the Domain and Centennial Park
in which to run.

If you are in the city in August, why
not join in the annual City to Surf fun
run from Sydney Town Hall to Bondi
Beach. The event attracts some 30,000
runners each year and is great fun.

ROCK SPORTS

Rock climbing, abseiling or canyoning
enthusiasts will find that there is plenty
of opportunity around Sydney. The Blue
Mountains are a haven for such sports.

Blue Mountains Climbing School,
Katoomba. _Tel: (047) 82 1271._

SKIING

Winter visitors should take advantage of
the good downhill, and excellent cross-
country, skiing opportunities available in
the Snowy Mountains area. The season
runs from June to early October, but the
best conditions are normally found from
July to mid-September.
Guthega Ski Resort. _Tel: (064) 57
5333._
Mt Blue Cow Ski Resort. _Tel: (008)
020 522._
Mt Selwyn Ski Resort. _Tel: (008) 020
777._
Perisher/Smiggins Resort. _Tel: (008)
020 700._
Thredbo Resort Centre. _Tel: 438 3122._

SQUASH

Squash courts are found in most Sydney
suburbs and country towns, and are
generally open for public hire for a
reasonable price. A central Sydney
squash centre is:
Hiscoe's Squash and Fitness Centre,
Surry Hills. _Tel: 699 3233._

TENNIS

The popularity of tennis in Australia has
been boosted by the fact that the game
can be played all year round. Some
central Sydney courts are:

Cooper Park Tennis, Double Bay. _Tel:
389 9259._
Jensen's Tennis Centre, Surry Hills.
Tel: 698 9451.
The Palms Tennis Centre,
Paddington. _Tel: 363 4955._

A leisurely game of bowls

Spectator Sports

*F*or those with the time and the inclination, there is much to enjoy as a spectator of Sydney's thriving sporting world. Information on what's happening and where is available in the back section of the daily papers, or call the numbers listed below.

BASKETBALL

This is an increasingly popular spectator sport, played from October to March. Most matches are held at the Sydney Entertainment Centre on Friday and Saturday evenings.

Sydney Entertainment Centre, City. *Tel: 211 2222.*

CRICKET

One of Australia's favourite spectator sports, cricket is played from October to March.

International and interstate matches are played at the famous Sydney Cricket Ground at Moore Park. Most matches take place at weekends, but week-day and floodlit evening play is also common.

Sydney Cricket Ground, Moore Park. *Tel: 360 6601.*

FOOTBALL/RUGBY

There are four codes to follow but, in Sydney, rugby league is by far and away the most popular. Major matches take place at the Sydney Football Ground at Moore Park on either Saturday or Sunday afternoons. Grand Finals of both league and union competitions are held in September.

Sydney Football Stadium, Moore Park. *Tel: 360 6601.*

Rugby union is also played on Saturdays. It's popular in Sydney, but on a much smaller scale than league.
Contact the Australian Rugby Football Union for details of matches. Tel: 662 1266.

Soccer and Australian Rules Football (*the* sport in Victoria!) have only a minority following in Sydney, but watching a match of the latter is an interesting and novel experience for the visitor.

Soccer

Contact the **Australian Soccer Federation** for details. *Tel: 597 6611.*

Australian Rules

Sydney Cricket Ground, Moore Park. *Tel: 332 3791.*

GOLF

The state's major professional tournament is the NSW Open, which is held in June at one of Sydney's top courses such as the Royal Sydney at Rose Bay.
Contact the Professional Golfers Association of Australia for details of events. Tel: 476 3333.

GREYHOUND RACING

This takes place at Glebe's Wentworth Park on most Monday and Saturday evenings.
Tel: 660 6232.

HORSE RACING

Australians are inveterate gamblers, and are passionate about this particular sport. Sydney has four excellent race courses, but Randwick, in the eastern suburbs, is the most convenient for visitors. The AJC Spring Racing Carnival, held in the first week of October, is a particularly exciting Randwick event. Other meetings rotate between the four courses and take place every Wednesday and Saturday.

Canterbury Racecourse. *Tel: 799 8000.*
Randwick Racecourse. *Tel: 663 8400.*
Rosehill Racecourse. *Tel: 682 1000.*
Warwick Farm Racecourse. *Tel: 602 6199.*

Sydney's Football Stadium

MOTOR RACING

The city's main motor racing venues are at Oran Park, in the southwest, and Amaroo Park, near Windsor. Most meetings are held on Sundays.

Amaroo Park Raceway, Annangrove. *Tel: 679 1121.*
Oran Park, Narellan. *Tel: (046) 46 1004.*

SAILING

From September to March the harbour is packed with racing boats. The most exciting events are the fast 18-foot skiff races, which take place on Saturday and Sunday afternoons. Spectator ferries leave from Circular Quay at 2pm. For visitors at Christmas-time, watching the start of the annual Sydney to Hobart yacht race on 26 December is a must! *For details of 18-footer races, contact the Sydney Flying Squadron. Tel: 955 8350.*

SURF CARNIVALS

Every visitor should enjoy a surf carnival. These are held on most weekends between October and March at Sydney's major surf beaches. Manly and Bondi are particularly good venues.
Surf Life Saving Association. *Tel: 597 5588.*

TENNIS

The tennis season is from October to February, with the major tournament being the New South Wales Open, which is played at White City every January. This event attracts major international stars and is well worth a visit. The Australian Indoor Championship is another important tournament: this takes place in October at the Sydney Entertainment Centre.
White City Tennis Club, Paddington. *Tel: 331 4144.*
Sydney Entertainment Centre, City. *Tel: 211 2222.*

TROTTING

Trotting (or harness racing) meetings are held on Tuesday and Friday nights at Harold Park Paceway in the city's inner east.
Harold Park Paceway, Glebe. *Tel: 660 3688.*

Food and Drink

*T*here is no doubt that Sydney is a diner's paradise! The Australian love for the good life, combined with the influx of immigrants from all over the world during the past 30 years, has produced a mouth-watering array of restaurants and cuisines often to be enjoyed outside. From Greek to Indian, Thai to Swiss and American to African, Sydney has the lot – and the standards are generally good to excellent. Cafés, especially Sydney's wonderful Italian coffee shops, and many English-style tea-shops, are also well-patronised and reasonably priced.

Although indigenous Australian food was once based on the traditions of bland English fare, there has been a recent, major improvement in menus. 'Oz Nouveau', or Modern Australian, has created a revolution in dining, with its light and innovative dishes based on seafood, meats and vegetables – all imaginatively presented.

There are prices to suit every pocket. One bonus of dining out in Australia is that many establishments (especially the lower-priced) are BYO – bring your own liquor.

With the fine selection of wines (prices ranging from A$6–25) and beers (from A$1.20 upwards) available, this policy makes eating out both inexpensive and enjoyable. Expect a corkage charge of A$1–3 if you bring your own liquor.

As a guide, prices can be divided into four approximate categories for a two-course meal with coffee (per person and not including alcohol):

$	A$10–12
$$	A$13–25
$$$	A$26–50
$$$$	A$50 plus

Licensed restaurants offer an excellent selection of wines, mostly Australian, with some French and other European, and prices per bottle starting at around A$12, zooming up to A$30 and more. Beer prices are reasonable anywhere and the selection includes some excellent Australian brews, as well as many European, Asian and American beers.

Service charges are rarely included in the bill and tipping is not compulsory, although 10 per cent is an acceptable gratuity, if you are happy with the food and service. Some restaurants add a small surcharge at weekends and public holidays. Major credit cards are widely accepted.

It is common for restaurants to close on Mondays, and some shut down on Sundays. Booking is recommended for any evening, but especially on Friday and Saturday nights. Restaurants in the city, The Rocks and other tourist spots are also likely to be busy at weekday lunchtimes.

Many of the lower-priced restaurants offer a takeaway service, with prices around 10 per cent cheaper than for dining in.

TOURIST RESTAURANTS
WITH A VIEW

Several restaurants have taken advantage of Sydney's spectacular setting. Remember, though, that people eat here more for the view than the brilliance of the cuisine.

$$$$ Bennelong Restaurant
International cuisine with views of the
city and water.
*Sydney Opera House. Tel: 250 7578. Train
or bus to Circular Quay.*

$$$ Sydney Tower Restaurants
Two revolving restaurants with
magnificent views. International cuisine.
*Centrepoint, corner of Pitt and Market
Streets, City. Tel: 233 3722.*

EXPENSIVE
If you feel like celebrating, or spending
big in elegant surroundings, Sydney has
much to offer in this category. Here are
some ideas.

$$$$ Berowra Waters Inn
Australia's best restaurant, on a
waterway north of Sydney. The best way
to get there is by seaplane – details from
the restaurant.
*Berowra Waters. Tel: 456 1027. By car or
seaplane.*

HOTEL RESTAURANTS
Sydney's five-star hotels offer fine food
and good service at $$$ to $$$$ prices:
all are licensed. Some suggestions are:

**Kables Restaurant, The Regent of
Sydney,**
199 George Street, City. Tel: 238 0000.
**Number 7 at The Park, Park Hyatt
Sydney Hotel,**
7 Hickson Road, The Rocks. Tel: 241 1234.
The Treasury, Hotel Inter-Continental,
117 Macquarie Street, City. Tel: 230 0200.

AUSTRALIAN FARE

$$$ Argyle Tavern
Traditional Australian food and the 'Jolly
Swagman' dinner show.

*18 Argyle Street, The Rocks. Tel: 247
7782. Bus or train to Circular Quay.*

$ Harry's Café de Wheels
Not a restaurant, but a pie stall and a
Sydney institution! Serves traditional
Aussie meat pies with peas and mashed
potato. BYO.
*1 Cowper Wharf Road, Woolloomooloo.
Open: 7am–3am. A short walk from
Kings Cross.*

CAFÉS AND COFFEE SHOPS
$ to $$ Art Gallery Café
Snacks, coffee and afternoon tea.
*Art Gallery of NSW, Art Gallery Road,
The Domain. Tel: 225 1700. A short walk
from the city centre.*

$ Bar Coluzzi
Sydney's best Italian coffee and snacks.
*322 Victoria Street, Darlinghurst. Tel: 380
5420. Train to Kings Cross.*

$ to $$ New Edition Tea Rooms
Great breakfasts and sandwiches.
*328a Oxford Street, Paddington. Tel: 361
0744. Bus 380 from Circular Quay/City.*

The Hard Rock Café in Crown Street

Gourmet Sydney

In recent years, the standard of Australian dining has taken a huge leap forward. English-style 'meat and three veg' is still popular with many families, but the dining-out choices, particularly in Sydney, are magnificent. Much of this variety and excellence is due to the influx of migrants, with their individual styles of cooking, from virtually every nation of the world, but thanks must also be given to the wonderful range of Australian produce that goes into these dishes.

Seafood is a prime example: exotic varieties of fish, huge prawns, oysters, mussels, crayfish (similar to lobster) and Tasmanian scallops grace many a seafood platter. Try some of these mouth-watering options – steamed ocean trout, char-grilled kingfish, tuna steaks or flathead in beer batter.

The array of fruit and vegetables is enough to make anyone turn vegetarian. Tropical fruits such as mangoes and papaya, or savoury choices like avocados, asparagus, sweet

Merivale's International Café in Woolloomooloo

There's plenty of choice for outdoor eating

potatoes and sun-dried tomatoes are all commonplace in Sydney's restaurants.

Many of these tempting ingredients go into the innovative indigenous cuisine which is dubbed 'Oz Nouveau'. Based on French-style *nouvelle cuisine*, this form of cooking is light, imaginative, low-fat and utterly delicious. Fish may be served with a tomato, basil and onion salsa, or slices of milk-fed lamb could be topped with an eggplant puree.

Thai food deserves a special mention. Many overseas visitors will not be familiar with this wonderful cuisine, which blends the freshest produce with chilli and delicate spices. The style is best summed up in one particular dish – *tom yum goong*. The essential ingredients of this soup are prawns, chilli, coriander and lemongrass: be assured, it's a taste sensation!

Fruits of the sea are a Sydney speciality

Café society is for all the family

Phillip's Foote Restaurant, The Rocks

City and East Sydney

AMERICAN
$$ Hard Rock Café
Hamburgers, club sandwiches and the like in a noisy, but fun, environment.
121 Crown Street, East Sydney. Tel: 331 1116. Bus 324/5 from Circular Quay to William Street.

CHINESE
$ Chinatown Centre
Eat well for around A$6 at this basic food court, which offers Chinese, Korean, Malaysian, Thai and Japanese fare.
25 Dixon Street, Chinatown. Tel: 212 3335. Train to Town Hall.

$$ Choys Inn
Good value and great food, including plenty of vegetarian dishes. Licensed BYO.
90–2 Hay Street, Chinatown. Tel: 211 4213. Train to Town Hall.

$$$ Imperial Peking
Sydney's best Chinese food in an up-market quayside setting.
15 Circular Quay West, The Rocks. Tel: 247 7073. Bus or train to Circular Quay.

In addition, Chinatown (the area around Dixon, Hay and Sussex Streets at the south end of the city) has innumerable Chinese restaurants that offer good, cheap food.

FRENCH
$$$ Claudines
This is fairly expensive, but lower-priced food is available in the adjoining café.
151 Macquarie Street, City. Tel: 241 1749. Train to Martin Place.

GREEK
$$ Diethnes
Sydney's longest-running Greek restaurant, which serves great food.
336 Pitt Street, City (between Bathurst and Liverpool Streets). Tel: 267 8956. Train to Museum Station.

INDIAN
$$ Indian Palace
Good Indian food, including a wide range of fish and vegetarian dishes.
266 Bourke Street, East Sydney. Tel: 331 3680. Bus 380 to Taylor Square.

INTERNATIONAL
$$ Soup Plus
Soup, pasta and meat dishes at low prices. Jazz bands play in the evenings: the place has a superb atmosphere.
383 George Street, City. Tel: 299 7728. Train to Town Hall.

ITALIAN
$ Bill and Toni
Unbelievably cheap Italian food, and a good downstairs coffee shop. BYO.
72–4 Stanley Street, East Sydney. Tel: 360 4702. Bus 389 from Circular Quay.

$$ Rossini
Delicious food and coffee with water views: outdoor tables.
Circular Quay. Tel: 247 8026. Bus or train to Circular Quay.

$$$ Tre Scalini
Stylish food and excellent service: booking is always essential here. Licensed.
174 Liverpool Street, East Sydney. Tel: 331 4358. Bus 380 from Circular Quay.

JAPANESE
$$ Origami
Excellent country-style Japanese food at low prices. Licensed BYO.
150 Liverpool Street, East Sydney. Tel: 331 3733. Bus 380 from Circular Quay.
$$$$ Suntory
Luxurious and expensive, with a beautiful garden setting.
529 Kent Street, City (between Bathurst and Liverpool Streets). Tel: 267 2900. Train to Town Hall.

MALAYSIAN/INDONESIAN
$$ Malaya
Fantastic food at cheap prices.
761 George Street, Haymarket. Tel: 211 4659. Train to Central Station.

MODERN AUSTRALIAN
$$$ to $$$$ Bilsons
Great location and wonderful food. It's expensive, but there is a good-value set-price lunch for around A$35.
Overseas Passenger Terminal, Circular Quay West. Tel: 251 5600. Bus or train to Circular Quay.

SEAFOOD
$$$ Doyles at the Quay
One of the famous Doyles' seafood restaurants – good food, great views.
Overseas Passenger Terminal, Circular Quay West. Tel: 252 3400. Train or bus to Circular Quay.
$$$ Jordons Seafood Restaurant
Fine seafood with water views.
Harbourside, Darling Harbour. Tel: 281 3711. Monorail from Pitt Street.
$$ Rockpool Oyster Bar
Seafood at reasonable prices and in pleasant surroundings. The Bar adjoins a more expensive restaurant.
109 George Street, The Rocks. Tel: 252 1888. Bus or train to Circular Quay.

SPANISH
$$ Capitan Torres
Specialises in seafood dishes and has a lively atmosphere.
73 Liverpool Street, City. Tel: 264 5574. Train to Town Hall.

THAI
$$$ Bangkok
Excellent service and food. One of Sydney's best Thai restaurants.
234 Crown Street, East Sydney. Tel: 361 4804. Bus 380 to Oxford Street.
$$ Prasit's on Crown
Another fine Thai restaurant.
273 Crown Street, East Sydney. Tel: 331 3026. Bus 380 to Oxford Street .

VEGETARIAN
$ to $$ Metro Café
Fantastic food, but open only for dinner from Wednesday to Friday, and Sunday. (No smoking.) BYO.
26 Burton Street, East Sydney. Tel: 361 5356.
$ El Sano
Excellent, cheap vegetarian food in the city centre. (No smoking.) BYO.
Shop 2, Colonial Mutual Arcade, corner of Pitt Street and Martin Place, City. Tel: 232 1304. Train to Martin Place.

The exotic Tai Pan restaurant

Eastern Suburbs and Inner West

*T*he Eastern Suburbs contain Sydney's best selection of restaurants, with Asian and Italian fare being particularly popular. With a few exceptions, most of the following eateries are in the Kings Cross, Darlinghurst and Paddington areas – all of these are a short distance from the city centre.

AMERICAN
$$ to $$$ Bourbon and Beefsteak
Open 24 hours, 365 days a year.
Breakfasts are particularly good.
24 Darlinghurst Road, Kings Cross.
Tel: 358 1144. Train or buses 324/5
to Kings Cross.

FRENCH
$$$$ Le Trianon
Classical French food and fine
surroundings.
29 Challis Avenue, Potts Point. Tel: 358
1353. Train or buses 324/5 to Kings Cross.

INDIAN
$$ Oh! Calcutta
A stylish restaurant serving mild Indian
food.
251 Victoria Street, Darlinghurst. Tel: 360
3650. Train to Kings Cross.

INDONESIAN
$$ Borobudur
Very popular (bookings essential on
weekends) and cheap. BYO.
263 Oxford Street, Darlinghurst. Tel: 331
3464. Bus 380 from Circular Quay.

ITALIAN
$$$ Atlanta
Serves excellent Italian food; fish dishes

are a speciality.
41 Crown Street, Woolloomooloo.
Tel: 361 6467. Bus 324/5 to William Street.
$$ Piccola Italia
A wonderful family-run establishment
that serves home-style Italian food.
481 Crown Street, Surry Hills. Tel: 699
4264. Taxi.

JAPANESE
$$$ Isaribi
Busy and noisy, with an unusual style of
Japanese food.
41 Elizabeth Bay Road, Elizabeth Bay.
Tel: 358 2125. Train to Kings Cross.

LEBANESE
$$ Azar
Another popular Sydney cuisine which is
cheap and worth sampling.
527 Crown Street, Surry Hills. Tel: 319
5682. Taxi.

MODERN AUSTRALIAN
$$ to $$$ Bayswater Brasserie
Innovative food in very pleasant
surroundings. Includes an outdoor
eating area.
32 Bayswater Road, Kings Cross. Tel: 357
2177. Train or bus 324/5 to Kings Cross.
$$ to $$$ Zigolinis
Open all day for anything from breakfast

to dinner or late evening snacks.
2 Short Street, Double Bay. Tel: 362 4282.
Bus 324/5 from Circular Quay.

SEAFOOD
$$$ Doyles on the Beach
Sydney's most famous seafood restaurant
with marvellous views of the harbour.
*11 Marine Parade, Watsons Bay. Tel: 337
2007. Bus 324/5 from Circular Quay.*
$$ Woolloomooloo Bay Hotel
Seafood, steaks and chips at pavement
tables with a harbour view.
*2 Bourke Street, Woolloomooloo. Tel: 357
1376. Bus 311 from Circular Quay.*

THAI
$$ Arun Thai
Fine Thai food and good service.
*13/39 Elizabeth Bay Road, Elizabeth Bay.
Tel: 357 7414. Train or bus 324/5 to
Kings Cross.*
$$ Narai Thai
A large and very popular Thai eatery.
*346 Victoria Street, Darlinghurst. Tel: 331
1390. Train to Kings Cross.*

VEGETARIAN
$ Govinda's
Unbelievably cheap, good food. Run by
the Hare Krishna Centre. (No alcohol
allowed, no smoking.)
*112 Darlinghurst Road, Darlinghurst.
Tel: 380 5162. Train to Kings Cross.*
$$ Laurie's
Fabulous veggie food at very reasonable
prices. (No-smoking area.) BYO.
*Corner of Victoria and Burton Streets,
Darlinghurst. Tel: 360 4915. Train to
Kings Cross.*

VIETNAMESE
$$ Chu Bay
Good food in a small, friendly
establishment. BYO.

*312a Bourke Street, Darlinghurst. Tel: 331
3386. Bus 380 to Taylor Square.*

INNER WEST

CAFÉ FOOD
$$ Caffe Troppo
Open from breakfast to dinner time –
has a pleasant outdoor dining area. (No-
smoking area.) BYO.
*175 Glebe Point Road, Glebe. Tel: 552
1233. Bus 431 from The Rocks or George
Street.*

INDIAN
$$ Manjit's
One of Sydney's better Indian restaurants.
*360 Darling Street, Balmain. Tel: 818 3681.
Bus 431 from The Rocks or George Street.*

ITALIAN
$$ to $$$ Numero Tre
Good food and service. BYO.
*159 Norton Street, Leichhardt. Tel: 560
9129. Bus 440 from Circular Quay.*

MODERN AUSTRALIAN
$$$ The Balmain Post
Up-market Oz Nouveau.
*1 Queen's Place, Balmain. Tel: 818 3380.
Bus 431 from The Rocks and George Street.*
$$$ Darling Mills
Imaginative food in a lovely old
sandstone building. (No-smoking area.)
*134 Glebe Point Road, Glebe. Tel: 660
5666. Bus 431 from The Rocks or
George Street.*

VIETNAMESE
$$ Kim-Van
Another Glebe Point Road eatery,
serving excellent Vietnamese food.
*147–9 Glebe Point Road, Glebe.
Tel: 660 5252. Bus 431 from The Rocks
or George Street.*

Suburban and Country Dining

SUBURBAN DINING

Out sightseeing away from the city, there are some excellent places to eat. Here are several suggestions.

BONDI BEACH

All of these are reached by train from Town Hall or Martin Place to Bondi Junction, then bus 380.

$$ Gelato Bar
Hungarian goulash, gelato, cakes and coffee. Very popular. BYO.
140 Campbell Parade. Tel: 30 4033.

$$ Lamrock Café
A splendid view over Bondi: serves everything from hearty breakfasts to evening meals. Licensed/BYO.
72 Campbell Parade. Tel: 30 6313.

$ to $$$ Ravesi's
Breakfasts, lunches and dinners with a lovely view of the parade and beach.
Corner of Campbell Parade and Hall Street. Tel: 365 4422.

LA PEROUSE

$$ to $$$ Danny's Seafood Restaurant
Good seafood in an ocean-front location near the Botany Bay attractions.
1605 Anzac Parade. Tel: 661 5055. Bus 394 from Circular Quay.

MANLY

Manly is reached by ferry or Jetcat from Circular Quay.

$$ Cafe Steyne
Excellent café fare at the south end of Manly Beach.
14 South Steyne. Tel: 977 0116.

$$ Nell's Restaurant
Great for breakfast.
Manly Pacific Parkroyal Hotel, 55 North Steyne. Tel: 977 7666.

NORTH SHORE

$$ Curry Bazaar
Indian and other Asian food at very reasonable prices. BYO.
334 Pacific Highway, Crows Nest. Tel: 436 3620. Bus 263 from Wynyard.

$$ to $$$ Duck's Crossing
Varied café-style food at lunchtime. More expensive at night. BYO.
12/7 Waters Road, Neutral Bay. Tel: 909 1593.Ferry from Circular Quay, then a connecting bus.

PALM BEACH AREA

It's best to drive here, but the northern beaches can also be reached by bus 190 from Wynyard.

$$$ Barrenjoey House
Modern Australian cuisine.
1108 Barrenjoey Road, Palm Beach. Tel: 974 4001.

$$ Boonchu Thai
One of the best Thai restaurants in northern Sydney. Licensed BYO.
Shop 8 Plaza Arcade, 343 Barrenjoey Road, Newport Beach. Tel: 997 3450.

PARRAMATTA

$$ City Extra Café
City Extra is open 24 hours and serves good café-style food and coffee. (No-smoking area.) Licensed/BYO.
301 Church Street, Parramatta. Tel: 633 1188. Train from Town Hall/Central.

COUNTRY DINING

Outside the Sydney region, the choice of restaurants and cuisines is far more limited.

BLUE MOUNTAINS
$ to $$ Bay Tree Tea Shop
The best café in the Mountains: home-style food is a speciality. BYO.
26 Station Street, Mount Victoria. Tel: (047) 87 1275.
$$$ Cleopatras
A guesthouse restaurant which is open to the public for lunch and dinner. French cuisine. BYO.
Cleopatra Street, Blackheath. Tel: (047) 87 8456.
$$ to $$$ Fairmont Resort
A choice of restaurants in the mountains' most up-market resort.
1 Sublime Point Road, Leura. Tel: (047) 82 5222.

CANBERRA
$$ Fringe Benefits Brasserie
French and Italian food in a brasserie setting.
54 Marcus Clarke Street, Canberra City. Tel: (06) 247 4042.
$$$ The Oak Room
Seafood and French dishes in Canberra's smartest hotel.
Hyatt Hotel, Commonwealth Avenue, Yarralumla. Tel: (06) 270 1234.

CENTRAL COAST
$$ to $$$ Peppers on Sea
A choice of restaurants in the Central Coast's finest resort.
Pine Tree Lane, Terrigal. Tel: (043) 84 9111.

NORTH COAST
These resorts all offer excellent food in their restaurants – all are licensed and in the $$ to $$$ range.
Deckchairs Bar & Grill, Nautilus on-the-beach, Coffs Harbour.
Tel: (066) 53 6699.
Pelican Beach Resort, Coffs Harbour.
Tel: (066) 53 7000.
Pelican Shores Resort Park Street, Port Macquarie. *Tel: (065) 83 3999.*

SNOWY MOUNTAINS
$ to $$$ Thredbo Resort Centre
A variety of cafés and restaurants in the Snowy Mountains' premier resort.
Thredbo Village. Tel: (064) 57 6360.

SOUTHERN HIGHLANDS
$$$ Milton Park
A Relais & Châteaux hotel with award-winning restaurant and wine cellar.
Horderns Road, Bowral. Tel: (048) 61 1522.

WINE AREAS
$$$ Peppers Restaurant
An award-winning hotel restaurant.
Peppers Hunter Valley Hotel, Ekerts Road, Pokolbin, Hunter Valley. Tel: (049) 98 7596.
$$$ Pokolbin Cellar Restaurant
Serves fine French-style food.
Hungerford Hill Wine Village, Broke Road, Pokolbin, Hunter Valley. Tel: (049) 98 7584.

The Corso at Manly

Drinking

Drinking is a popular social event in Sydney – be it in one of the city's many colourful hotels (pubs), in a cosmopolitan cocktail bar, or the luxurious surroundings of a five-star hotel. There is a great variety of beers: European, American and Asian brands are sold alongside an ever-widening range of Australian brews. In addition to the well-known Fosters, Swan and XXXX brands, try some of the more unusual, boutique-style offerings such as Hahn, Redback, Cascade, Thunderbolt or Brewers. Beer is served in middies (small glasses), schooners (large glasses) and by the can or bottle.

All pubs and bars also serve the usual range of spirits, as well as Australian red, white and sparkling wines. If possible, opt for bottled wine, rather than the cheaper cask variety. Drinks prices, except in the most exclusive hotel and cocktail bars, are very reasonable.

The sign of the famous Lord Nelson Hotel

PUBS

Hotels are licensed to trade for 12 hours a day, with most opening from 11am to 11pm. Late-night drinking is permitted in many hotels and cocktail bars. The minimum age for drinking alcohol is 18 years and children are welcome only in pubs with beer gardens or other oudoor areas.

CITY
Hero of Waterloo
Small, atmospheric, and licensed since 1845.
81 Windmill Street, Miller's Point.
Lord Nelson
Sydney's oldest hotel, licensed since 1842. Excellent restaurant upstairs.
19 Kent Street, Miller's Point.
Mercantile Hotel
Sydney's premier Irish pub.
25 George Street, The Rocks.
The Orient Hotel
A nicely renovated pub, with live jazz on Saturday and Sunday afternoons.
89 George Street, The Rocks.
Pumphouse Brewery Tavern
An historic building with an excellent range of boutique beers.
17 Little Pier Street, Darling Harbour.

EASTERN SUBURBS
Albury Hotel
Sydney's premier gay pub with drag shows, a piano bar and a good Thai restaurant.
6 Oxford Street, Paddington.
Dolphin Hotel
An outdoor courtyard, plus excellent, reasonably priced lunch and dinner menus.
412 Crown Street, Surry Hills.

Four in Hand
A busy, well-renovated hotel and restaurant: pleasant, but trendy.
Corner of Sutherland and Elizabeth Streets, Paddington.

Lord Dudley
An English-style pub which is popular with an older age group. There is also a downstairs courtyard restaurant.
Corner Jersey and Quarry Roads, Woollahra.

Royal Hotel
In the heart of trendy Paddington – very lively and popular.
237 Glenmore Road, Paddington.

Watsons Bay Hotel
Well known for its beer garden and harbour views. Especially good for weekend barbecue and seafood lunches.
1 Military Road, Watsons Bay.

Woolloomooloo Bay Hotel
Live music most nights in a waterfront location: it gets very crowded.
2 Bourke Street, Woolloomooloo.

NORTH SHORE
The Oaks Hotel
The centre of north shore drinking: also has good value barbecue-your-own food.
118 Military Road, Neutral Bay.

HOTEL BARS
Hotel Inter-Continental
Several options here, but aim for the Treasury Bar – on the 31st floor. It has great views.
117 Macquarie Street, City.

The Regent of Sydney
Several up-market bars in the city's finest hotel.
199 George Street, City.

The Ritz-Carlton
A choice of pleasant places to drink in.
93 Macquarie Street, City.

Sydney Hilton International
Famous for its marvellous, ornate

Marble Bar in the basement.
259 Pitt Street, City.

COCKTAIL AND WINE BARS

CITY
Bobby McGee's
Cocktails, food and dancing until late.
Harbourside, Darling Harbour.

Scarlett's Cellar
Open until midnight, with live entertainment.
Harbour Rocks Hotel, 34–52 Harrington Street, The Rocks.

EASTERN SUBURBS
Back Door
A popular café which also has a nice bar area. Trendy.
231a Victoria Street, Darlinghurst.

Barons
Drink until very late in a relaxed atmosphere.
5 Roslyn Street, Kings Cross.

Bourbon and Beefsteak
Open 24 hours for food, music and drinks.
Darlinghurst Road, Kings Cross.

Kinselas
There are two pleasant bars here, plus live theatre and cabaret.
383 Bourke Street, Taylor Square, Darlinghurst.

COUNTRY DRINKING
All NSW country towns are well served by pubs. Although some may be a little rough and ready, they are always full of local colour. Unless an establishment looks particularly unsavoury, just take pot luck and plunge in! Additionally, beach and country resorts in all areas have more sophisticated bars which are generally open to the public. (See also Country Dining).

Hotel Tips

*A*lthough the standard of Australian hotels is generally high, visitors should be aware that the tradition of service is not one that is ingrained in the Australian nature. Except in the very best hotels, do not expect the same standards of service that are found in Asian, American or European establishments.

SYDNEY HOTELS
There is a Sydney hotel to suit every budget: from the international standard of the Regent of Sydney, the city's very best, to three-star establishments, serviced apartments for families, youth hostels and innumerable backpackers' lodges.

The majority of Sydney's hotels are located in the city and inner eastern suburbs – particularly around Kings Cross and Elizabeth Bay: these are very convenient locations for sightseeing. Suburban tourist centres such as Manly, Bondi Beach and Parramatta also have a good range of places in which to stay.

COUNTRY HOTELS
Country areas of NSW offer a wide range of accommodation standards. Some towns and cities will have only the local unsophisticated, but comfortable, motel, while large coastal towns and the more popular inland destinations provide a very high standard of hotels and resorts. The Blue Mountains, Hunter Valley and Southern Highlands, for example, have some excellent, up market, resorts and guesthouses.

Bookings and peak periods
Peak holiday times in New South Wales are from Christmas to the end of January, and at Easter time – both of these are major school holiday periods. At these times, accommodation is very heavily booked, so plan your itinerary

well in advance if you are visiting then. If you need assistance in selecting or booking any Sydney or NSW country accommodation, contact the NSW Travel Centre in Sydney on 231 4444.

ACCOMMODATION CATEGORIES
Prices
The more expensive Sydney hotels publish a room-only price, whereas breakfast is usually included in the tariff of smaller establishments. Motels, youth hostels and backpackers' lodges are always on a room-only basis. The prices below are approximate only, and unless otherwise indicated are for twin/double rooms, per night.

Deluxe ($250 plus)
Into this category fall international-standard hotels such as the Regent of Sydney, the Inter-Continental, Park Hyatt, Sheraton Wentworth, Sebel Town House and Hotel Nikko. These are Sydney's very best establishments, and charge accordingly.

Premier ($150–$240)
The Hyatt Kingsgate at Kings Cross, the Manly Pacific Parkroyal, the Old Sydney Parkroyal and Harbour Rocks Hotel at The Rocks, and the Savoy Double Bay are some examples of this category. They offer top-class accommodation at more affordable prices.

Moderate ($90–$140)

There is plenty to choose from in this category of comfortable, but not luxurious, accommodation: the Gazebo Ramada, Sheraton Motor Hotel and Clairmont Inn at Kings Cross are examples.

Budget ($50–$80)

Many hotels in the city centre and around Kings Cross (such as the Manhattan), as well as numerous pubs, offer basic but adequate rooms for the budget traveller. Most of these will be on a shared bathroom basis.

OTHER TYPES OF ACCOMMODATION

This ranges from basic but comfortable youth hostels, to bed-and-breakfast in a 19th-century historic house.

Backpackers' Lodges

$15–$30 per person

Most of these are found in Kings Cross and Potts Point, Sydney's backpacker land. Such basic lodges usually offer both dormitory-style and private room accommodation and are very much for the budget-conscious traveller.

Bed-and-Breakfast/ Homestay

$70–$120

This is an economical alternative and a good way to meet the locals. In country areas of NSW it is also possible to stay on farms and rural properties. Contact the NSW Farm and Country Association on (066) 538408.

Boutique Hotels and Guesthouses

$90–$150

These small establishments provide bed-and-breakfast, usually in old homes and buildings of great character. The Russell, in The Rocks, and The Kendall and The Jackson at Potts Point are some good examples.

Country Motels

$70–$100

Drive-in motels (park your car outside your room) are an Australian institution and are particularly common in NSW country areas. Many of these offer family rooms, which are excellent value for the budget-conscious traveller.

Serviced Apartments

$90–$160

There is a large number of these moderately priced establishments in Sydney. They all have more than one bedroom, with cooking facilities, and are ideal for families or those travelling in small groups.

Youth Hostels

$12–$20 per person

Sydney has four youth hostels – at Pittwater, Dulwich Hill and two in the Glebe area, near Sydney University, providing low-cost dormitory and twin-share accommodation for YHA members.

The up-market Regent Hotel

Practical Guide

CONTENTS
Arriving
Camping
Children
Climate
Conversion Table
Crime
Customs
   Regulations
Disabled Travellers
Driving
Electricity
Embassies and
   Consulates
Emergency
   Telephone
   Numbers
Etiquette
Health
Hitch-hiking
Insurance
Language
Lost Property

Maps
Media
Money Matters
National Holidays
Opening Hours
Organised Tours
Pharmacies
Photography
Places of Worship
Police
Post Offices
Public Transport
Sport
Student and Youth
   Travel
Telephones
Ticket Agencies
Time
Tipping
Toilets
Tourist Offices
Valeting/Laundry

ARRIVING

All visitors require a valid passport and, except for holders of New Zealand passports, a valid visa to enter Australia.

By air

Sydney's airport is served by around 45 international passenger and cargo airlines, from Europe, North America, Asia, the Pacific and Africa. Australian customs and quarantine regulations are notoriously strict (see page 179). The arrivals area contains a café, bank, tourist information service, telephones and car hire desks. Baggage lockers are available, and the airport also has an inbound duty-free shop.

Sydney's Kingsford Smith Airport is just 12km from the city centre. Taxis are plentiful, and not too expensive. Journey time to the city centre is approximately 30 minutes. State Transit bus no 300 runs from the International Terminal to Circular Quay, via the Domestic Terminal, Central Railway and Town Hall, while no 350 operates to the Domestic Terminal, Central Station, Kings Cross and Elizabeth Bay. *Recorded airport international arrival and departure information is available on 00555 1850.*

By ship

Arriving by ship is rare these days, and it is generally only those who are on a cruise who will enter the country in this manner.

By train

Sydney's Central Railway Station is located just a few minutes south of the city centre. Taxis are readily available: alternatively, visitors arriving from other states or NSW country areas can easily transfer from the country trains area to suburban platforms.

Departing

All departing passengers over the age of 12 years must pay A$20 departure tax (in cash, in Australian currency). Passengers must check in at least one and a half hours before their flight departure time. Duty-free and souvenir shops are located in the check-in area, and also once you have passed through immigration.

CAMPING

It is not possible to camp anywhere in the central Sydney area, but several caravan/camping sites are located within 16km of the city centre:

Meriton Tourist Park, North Ryde. *Tel: 887 2177.*
Ramsgate Beach Tourist Park, Ramsgate. *Tel: 529 7257.*
Sheralee Tourist Caravan Park, Rockdale. *Tel: 567 7161.*

Many of NSW's national parks permit camping. Contact the National Parks and Wildlife Service on *585 6333* (8.30am–4.30pm) for details of any park.
Equipment hire
Eagle Hire, Artarmon. *Tel: 436 2016.*
Southern Cross Equipment, City. *Tel: 261 3435.*

CHILDREN

There is plenty to entertain children, but be particularly alert when they are in the water (treacherous currents and marine stingers), and in the strong summer sun. Make sure that they are protected with insect repellent, particularly in the evenings. Family discounts are often available on public transport and for museum entrances.

CLIMATE

Australian seasons are the reverse of those in the northern hemisphere. Summer is from December to February, autumn from March to May, winter from June to August, and Spring comes between September and November.

Sydney has a warm temperate climate, with a warm (which can become hot) summer. Rain is most likely to fall in June and the other winter months, and is least likely in September.

New South Wales is a large state and temperatures vary considerably. Essentially, the north is warmer and often wetter than Sydney; the south is slightly cooler; and the outback experiences extremes from cool to very hot. Highland regions such as the Great Dividing Range have colder winters, with snow on the latter for around three months of the year.

Weather Chart Conversion
25.4mm = 1 inch
$°F = 1.8 × °C + 32$

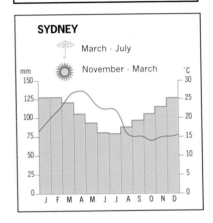

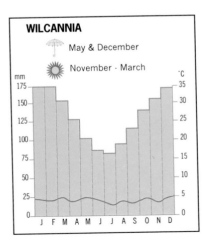

CONVERSION TABLE

FROM	TO	MULTIPLY BY
Inches	Centimetres	2.54
Centimetres	Inches	0.3937
Feet	Metres	0.3048
Metres	Feet	3.2810
Yards	Metres	0.9144
Metres	Yards	1.0940
Miles	Kilometres	1.6090
Kilometres	Miles	0.6214
Acres	Hectares	0.4047
Hectares	Acres	2.4710
Gallons	Litres	4.5460
Litres	Gallons	0.2200
Ounces	Grams	28.35
Grams	Ounces	0.0353
Pounds	Grams	453.6
Grams	Pounds	0.0022
Pounds	Kilograms	0.4536
Kilograms	Pounds	2.205
Tons	Tonnes	1.0160
Tonnes	Tons	0.9842

A young customer at Manly Cove's fairground

Children love Australia

Men's Suits

UK		36	38	40	42	44	46	48
Rest of Europe	46	48	50	52	54	56	58
US		36	38	40	42	44	46	48

Dress Sizes

UK		8	10	12	14	16	18
France		36	38	40	42	44	46
Italy		38	40	42	44	46	48
Rest of Europe	34	36	38	40	42	44
US		6	8	10	12	14	16

Men's Shirts

UK	14	14.5	15	15.5	16	16.5	17
Rest of Europe	36	37	38	39/40	41	42	43
US	14	14.5	15	15.5	16	16.5	17

Men's Shoes

UK	7	7.5	8.5	9.5	10.5	11
Rest of Europe	41	42	43	44	45	46
US	8	8.5	9.5	10.5	11.5	12

Women's Shoes

UK	4.5	5	5.5	6	6.5	7
Rest of Europe	38	38	39	39	40	41
US	6	6.5	7	7.5	8	8.5

Captain Cook cruises in the harbour

CRIME

Although crime is increasing and it always pays to keep an eye on your valuables, Sydney is a relatively safe city. If you do experience a theft or an attack, report it to your hotel and/or the police. If your travellers' cheques are stolen, report the theft to the organisation recommended in the information supplied when you purchased your cheques. Lost or stolen Thomas Cook Travellers' cheques must be reported by telephone to the Thomas Cook refund emergency number (see page 181). Emergency local assistance can also be obtained from Thomas Cook branches and *bureaux de change* (see page 184).

Cruises on offer at Circular Quay

CUSTOMS REGULATIONS

Customs and quarantine regulations are notoriously strict. Australia is free of many vegetable and animal diseases and pests and the importation of all goods of human, animal or plant origin is rigidly controlled. Any such items must be declared on the form provided on your in-bound aircraft. Penalties for drug importation offences are severe, and it is illegal to import items such as ivory and products from endangered species.

Adult visitors are permitted to bring in one litre of liquor and 250 cigarettes, plus other dutiable goods to the value of A$400 per person. There is no limit on the amount of funds for personal use.

One of the Sydney Explorer's stops

DISABLED TRAVELLERS

Australia is very aware of the needs of disabled people, and full information is available from **Australia Council for Rehabilitation of the Disabled (ACROD)**, *tel: 809 4405*; and the **Advisory Service for the Handicapped**, *tel: 918 9770*.

Sydney's international airport

DRIVING

Overseas driving licences are valid throughout NSW, although it is preferable to have an international permit.

The standard of road surfaces varies considerably: city roads and highways are generally good, but many outback and country roads are unsealed. The state's accident statistics are nothing to be proud of, so take care.

Regulations

Drive on the left and overtake on the right. Speed limits vary from 60kph in built-up areas to 100kph on other roads and freeways (110kph on certain designated freeways). It is compulsory to wear seat belts in both front and rear seats. Drink-driving laws are very strict in NSW, and random breath-testing is a common occurrence.

Full details of regulations and road signs are available from the **NRMA** (National Roads and Motorists Association) at 151 Clarence Street, Sydney *(Tel: 260 9222)*. This organisation can also assist with road maps, tour planning and general motoring information. Members of most international motoring associations are entitled to receive reciprocal service arrangements with the NRMA.

Breakdowns

The NRMA offers a 24-hour emergency breakdown service. *Tel: 13 1111.*

Petrol

Petrol, or gas, is sold by the litre and comes in regular, super, diesel and unleaded varieties. Prices are very reasonable compared with many countries.

Vehicle hire

You must be over 21 to hire a car – note that compulsory third party insurance is included in rental prices.

Cars

There are innumerable car hire outlets in Sydney and throughout NSW. Some of the most reliable are:

Avis	*Tel: 516 2877*
Hertz	*Tel: 008 333 377*
Thrifty	*Tel: 357 5399*

Drive carefully - koala warning sign

Campervans, motor-homes and four-wheel drive vehicles

Brits Rentals	Tel: 540 3321
Budget	Tel: 13 2848
Newmans	
Campervans	Tel: 597 3686

Motorcycles

All Bike Hire	Tel: 707 1691
Maverick	
Motorcycles	Tel: 746 2005/2006

Parking in Oxford Street, Paddington

Chauffeur-driven services

Ace Vintage	
Rentals	Tel: 328 1444
Budget Chauffeur	
Drive	Tel: 693 5500
Hughes Chauffeured	
Limousines	Tel: 693 2833

Some Thomas Cook *bureaux de change* offer car-hire (see page 184).

ELECTRICITY

The electric current in Australia is 240–250 volts AC and a flat three-pin adapter will be required for most non-Australian appliances. Hotels provide 110-volt shaver sockets.

EMBASSIES AND CONSULATES

Embassies are located in Canberra, the national capital, but consular representation is available in Sydney on the following telephone numbers:

Canada	Tel: 231 6522
New Zealand	Tel: 233 8388
UK	Tel: 247 9731
US	Tel: 261 9200

For Ireland, telephone Canberra *(06) 273 3022* as there is no representation in Sydney.

EMERGENCY TELEPHONE NUMBERS

Ambulance, Police and Fire Brigade services can all be contacted by dialling 000. Other useful Sydney (02) numbers :
Chemist Emergency Prescription Service *Tel: 438 3333*
Crisis Centre *Tel: 358 6577*
Dental Emergency Information *Tel: 267 5919*
Life Line *Tel: 264 2222*
Motoring breakdowns: see Driving
St Vincent's Public Hospital (Accident & Emergency) *Tel: 361 2520*
Sydney Hospital *Tel: 228 2111*
Thomas Cook travellers' cheques refund (24-hour service): Melbourne (3) 696 – 2952 (reverse charges).

ETIQUETTE

Australia is a very relaxed country and the visitor is unlikely to make social blunders, except perhaps by being too formal! The only exception may be smoking, which is becoming increasingly socially unacceptable. No-smoking zones on public transport, in restaurants, cinemas, theatres and other areas are well marked. The dress code is generally smart-casual for all occasions except the most formal. Topless sunbathing is widely accepted.

Vital protection against the fierce sun

HEALTH
Regulations
Proof of vaccination against diseases such as yellow fever, cholera and typhoid is required only if you are arriving from an infected area.

Health care
Australian health care standards are very high and hospitals and doctors are readily available. Overseas visitors, however, are not covered by the government-operated Medicare service, and ambulance, medical and dental services are quite expensive, so take out a health insurance policy before you leave home. British passport holders are entitled to basic emergency medical and hospital treatment, under a reciprocal arrangement.

Pharmacies sell a wide range of unrestricted drugs over the counter, but if you require antibiotics or stronger drugs, a doctor's prescription is necessary. Visitors are permitted to import up to four weeks' supply of prescribed medications, but if you wish to bring more you should obtain a doctor's certificate to avoid any potential problems with Customs.

If travelling on to Asia or other countries, the **Traveller's Medical and Vaccination Centre** *(Tel: 221 7133)* provides the best information and service.

Health problems
The worst problems that most visitors will encounter are sunburn and mosquito or sandfly bites. In summer, wear a hat and factor 15 sun block and don't spend too long in the sun. You should also protect yourself, particularly in the evenings, with an insect repellent such as Rid or Aerogard. Tap water is safe to drink in all NSW towns. AIDS is on the increase in Australia, particularly Sydney, so protect yourself in sexual encounters.

HITCH-HIKING
Although this is not illegal in NSW, it is discouraged by the police. Generally it is not too hard to get a lift, especially if you are travelling long distances, but be cautious about who picks you up: common sense should always prevail. Hitch-hiking is not permitted on freeways.

INSURANCE
Before leaving home, take out travel insurance for medical treatment and loss or theft of your possessions. If you are hiring a vehicle while in Australia, compulsory third-party insurance is included in the rental.

LANGUAGE
English is spoken in Australia, but it has been adapted and modified to form 'Strine', a uniquely colourful, informal and abbreviated version of the mother tongue.

Here are some commonly used words and expressions.

arvo	afternoon
barbie	barbecue
beaut	very good, great
bottle shop	off-licence
chook	chicken
cozzie	bathing costume
crook	sick, no good
daggy	dreadful (as in unfashionable)
daks	trousers
dero	derelict/tramp
dinky di	the real thing
dunny	toilet
fair dinkum	genuine
g'day	hello (a universal greeting)
garbo	garbage collector
grog	alcohol
lob up	arrive
mate	universal salutation (mostly male)
middy	small beer glass
mozzie	mosquito
ocker	classic Aussie male loudmouth
Oz	Australia
plonk	cheap wine
pom	English person
ratbag	offbeat person
ratshit	ruined, useless
ripper	good, great
schooner	large beer glass
she'll be right	it'll all be OK
shoot through	to leave
shout	a round of drinks
snags	sausages
spunky	good looking, sexy
ta	thank you
tea	evening meal
togs	swimming costume
tucker	food
ute	utility, pick-up truck
whinge	complain
wimp	spineless person
youse	plural of you

LOST PROPERTY

Call the **State Rail Authority**
(tel: 211 4535) or **State Transit**
(tel: 256 4666) lost property offices if you
have left an item on trains, buses or
ferries, and the relevant taxi company for
losses in cabs. In other circumstances,
loss or theft should always be reported
to, and later checked with, the police.

The city is well signposted

MAPS

The New South Wales Travel Centre
can supply free maps of the central
Sydney area and The Rocks (see Tourist
Offices for address). Other reasonably
priced maps can be purchased from any
bookshop and some newsagents. City
transport maps are available from Urban
Transit offices at major railway stations
such as Town Hall and Central.

Bearing all at carnival time

View of old Luna Park

MEDIA
Newspapers and magazines
Sydney's best daily paper is *The Sydney Morning Herald,* which includes a television guide on Mondays and a useful entertainment guide on Fridays. The other daily paper is the *Daily Telegraph Mirror,* while *The Australian* is a good national paper. The tabloid-style *Sunday Telegraph* and *Sun-Herald* are published on Sundays. Australians are avid magazine readers and visitors will find publications on topics from computers to composting. The weekly *Bulletin* is Australia's answer to *Time* and *Newsweek* magazines.

Radio
Again, plenty of choice – from the FM rock music stations such as 2 DAY-FM, 2 JJJ-FM and 2MMM-FM, to the Australian Broadcasting Corporation (ABC) operated Radio National and 2 BL. There are also a host of AM music, chat and news stations.

Television
Sydney has five television channels, including commercial-free ABC Channel 2 and SBS, the excellent multi-cultural station. Channels 7, 9 and 10 are commercially operated and provide the usual news, soap operas and mass-viewing fare. Outside Sydney, some channels are restricted, but all areas of NSW receive ABC transmissions. Clubs, pubs and some other establishments subscribe to the pay-TV station, Sky channel, which mainly features innumerable sports programmes.

MONEY MATTERS
There is no limit on the amount of personal funds that visitors may bring into Australia, and it is not necessary to keep exchange receipts.

Banks and currency exchange
Banks are generally open from 9.30am to 4pm Monday to Friday, with a one-hour extension to 5pm on Fridays. Major city banks open from 8.15am to 5pm on weekdays. Money-changing outlets such as Thomas Cook are generally open from 9am to 5pm Monday to Saturday, with many also operating on Sundays. Airport exchange facilities are open daily from 5.30am to 11pm.

Thomas Cook branches with *bureaux de change* are located as follows: 175 Pitt Street, GPO; Shop 222, Lower Ground Floor, Queen Victoria Building, George Street; Shop 509, Hyatt Kingsgate Shopping Centre, corner of Darlinghurst/Kings Cross; Management Centre, 3rd Floor, 95–9 York Street; 13th Floor, Forestry House, 95–9 York Street. All except the last office have foreign exchange facilities and can provide help in the event of lost or stolen Thomas Cook travellers' cheques. The first two offices also offer excursions and car rental.

Credit cards

These are widely accepted. The most useful are Visa, MasterCard, Bankcard and American Express.

Currency

Australia's decimal currency system is comprised of dollars, which are made up of 100 cents. Banknotes are brightly coloured and come in 5, 10, 20, 50 and 100 dollar denominations. Coins include A\$2, A\$1 (both gold-coloured), 50 cents, 20 cents, 10 cents and 5 cents (silver coloured). The copper 1 and 2 cent coins are currently being phased out of use.

Travellers' cheques

Most major varieties are widely accepted. Thomas Cook Australian dollars travellers' cheques can be cashed at banks, hotels, tourist centres and many shops. They can also be cashed free of commission charge at branches of Thomas Cook with foreign exchange facilities (see opposite).

NATIONAL HOLIDAYS

All banks, post offices, government and private offices and most shops and stores close on public holidays. Public transport operates on these days, but on a restricted Sunday-type service.

New South Wales Holidays

1 January, New Year's Day; 4th Monday in January, Australia Day; Easter; 25 April, Anzac Day; 2nd Monday in June, Queen's Birthday; 1st Monday in August, Bank Holiday (banks only) 1st Monday in October, Labour Day; Christmas Day; Boxing Day.

The summer school holidays run from mid-December to late January and at this time hotels and all tourist facilities become very heavily booked. The Easter holiday (usually early to mid-April) is also a very busy period.

OPENING HOURS

Banks

See Money Matters.

Museums and Galleries

These generally open from 10am to 5pm daily, but check, as some close on one day of the week.

Post Offices

See below.

Restaurants

A large proportion of restaurants close on Mondays.

Shops

Generally 9am to 5.30pm Monday to Friday, with late night shopping until 9pm on Thursdays. Saturday hours are normally 9am to 4pm and some large and department stores open on Sundays until 4pm. Suburban grocery and corner shops often stay open daily from 8am to 8pm or later.

Sydney's once popular Luna Park

ORGANISED TOURS

See also Sport on pages 156–61 for
activities such as scuba diving, horse
riding, rock climbing and skiing.

General Tour Operators

The following operators run coach and
other sightseeing trips around the
Sydney region:

AAT King's Tours *Tel: 252 2788*
Clipper Tours *Tel: 241 3983*
Australian Pacific Tours
Tel: 252 2988

Adventure Travel Operators

The following all specialise in outdoor
activities – including white-water rafting,
rock sports, cycling and bushwalking:
Peregrine Adventures *Tel: 231 3588*
Waratah Adventure Safaris
Tel: 419 7716
Wild Escapes *Tel: 247 2133*
Wilderness Expeditions *Tel: 956 8099*
The Wilderness Society *Tel: 267 7929*
Youth Hostels Association of NSW
Tel: 267 3044

Boat Cruises

The following operate cruises on Sydney
Harbour:
Bounty Cruises (tall ship)
Tel: 247 1789
Captain Cook Cruises *Tel: 251 5007*
Matilda Cruises *Tel: 264 7377*
Solway Lass (tall ship) *Tel: 264 7377*
Sydney Ferries *Tel: 954 4422*

Boat Hire

Sydney Harbour:
Charter Boat Information Service
Tel: 898 0395
Eastsail *Tel: 327 1166*
Flagship Charters *Tel: 327 4999*
Sail Australia *Tel: 957 2577*

Pittwater and Hawkesbury River:
Able Hawkesbury River Houseboats
Tel: (045) 66 4308
Holidays-A-Float *Tel: 985 7368*
Luxury Afloat *Tel: 985 7344*
Pittwater Yacht Charter: *Tel: 997
5344*
Murray River:
Aquavilla Houseboats (Wentworth)
Tel: (008) 039 094
Luxury Afloat (Moama)
Tel: (054) 82 5177
Myall Lakes:
Luxury Afloat *Tel: 985 7344*
Myall Lakes Houseboats
Tel: (049) 97 4221
Tea Gardens Houseboats and
Cruisers *Tel: (049) 97 0555*

Canoeing

Great Lakes Canoe Tours (Myall
Lakes) *Tel: (049) 92 2076*

Farm Holidays

NSW Farm and Country Holiday
Association *Tel: (066) 53 8408*

Horse Riding Holidays

Blue Mountains:
Boomerang Trail Rides
Tel: (047) 82 4560
The Packsaddlers: *Tel: (047) 87 9150*
Canberra:
Menzels Bushventures
Tel: (06) 281 6682
Myall Lakes:
Myall Lakes Horse Back Adventures
Tel: (049) 97 4511
Snowy Mountains:
Reynella Rides *Tel: (008) 029 909*
Talbingo Trails *Tel: (064) 54 2229*
South Coast:
Oaks Ranch and Country Club (near
Batemans Bay) *Tel: (044) 71 7403*
Southern Highlands:

Tugalong Station *Tel: (048) 78 9247*
Skiing Holidays
Alpine Tours International
Tel: 411 1033
Snowy Mountains Reservation
Centre *Tel: (008) 020 622*

Surfing Holidays
The Surf Travel Company
Tel: 527 4722/4119

Wildlife
See page 155 for details of wildlife parks.

PHARMACIES
Most pharmacies follow normal
shopping hours, but those in tourist
areas such as Kings Cross, The Rocks
and Darling Harbour are often open late
into the evening. See also Emergency
Telephone Numbers for the after-hours
prescription service.

Pharmacies and chemist's shops
stock everything from cosmetics to panty
hose, contraceptives, nappies, travellers'
items and film. Mild drugs such as
Panadeine, aspirin and cough medicines
are freely available. Other drugs require
a doctor's prescription.

PHOTOGRAPHY
Print and slide film can be purchased
from camera shops, pharmacies and
other stores and is not too expensive. It
is a good idea, though, to stock up on
duty-free supplies before arriving. Print
film processing is fast, readily available
and usually good-quality, while Kodak
or Fuji slide film will generally take three
to five days.

PLACES OF WORSHIP
Anglican:
St Andrew's Cathedral, George Street,
City (next to the Town Hall).

Baptist:
Central Baptist Church, 619 George
Street, City.
Inter-denominational:
Wayside Chapel, 29 Hughes Street,
Kings Cross.
Jewish:
The Great Synagogue, 189 Elizabeth
Street, City.
Muslim:
Telephone the Islamic Council of NSW
for details: 742 5752.
Roman Catholic:
St Mary's Cathedral, College Street,
City.
Presbyterian:
Scots Church, 44 Margaret Street.

POLICE
NSW police wear dark blue and pale
blue uniforms and a peaked, flat-topped
cap. They are generally helpful and
polite.

In cases of emergency, the police can
be contacted by telephoning 000, but for
general enquiries or assistance call the
City of Sydney Police Station on 265
6499 (24-hour service)

POST OFFICES
Sydney's General Post Office (GPO) is
located in Martin Place, between Pitt
and George Streets. The GPO is open
from 8.15am to 5.30pm Monday to
Friday, and 8.30am to 12 noon on
Saturdays. All other offices follow the
Monday to Friday, 9am to 5pm routine.
Services offered include stamps,
aerogrammes, telegrams and lettergrams,
while larger offices provide facsimile and
electronic post facilities. The best
Sydney *poste restante* address is c/o GPO
Martin Place, Sydney, NSW 2000. All
major country towns and most city
suburbs have their own post offices.

PUBLIC TRANSPORT
Timetable information
Sydney rail, bus and ferry route and timetable information is available from Metrotrips (tel: 954 4422) from 6am to 10pm daily.

Discount tickets and special services
The Sydneypass is an economical three-day ticket which is valid for the Airport Express Bus, Sydney Explorer Bus, normal bus services, ferries and special ferry cruises.

Buses (metropolitan)
MetroTen bus tickets are valid for 10 bus journeys at a greatly reduced rate. BusTripper tickets provide unlimited one day bus travel. A special tourist service operates on the Sydney Explorer Bus. This frequent service travels on a continuous 20km loop, stopping at 22 of the city's top sightseeing attractions. Passengers are provided with a commentary, and can board when and where they like during the course of one day. Details are available from Metrotrips.

Ferries
FerryTen tickets provide 10 harbour trips at a greatly discounted rate.

Rail
Off-peak travel tickets save up to 50 per cent and are valid for travel in the Sydney Metropolitan Area after 9am on weekdays, or at any time on weekends and public holidays. The Cityhopper ticket permits unlimited one-day train travel in the inner city area, after 9am on weekdays and all day at weekends.

For information on long distance rail and coach travel, as well as related accommodation bookings and general advice, call Countrylink on 217 8812.

Airlines
The major domestic airlines, which fly both within NSW and interstate, are:

Air NSW	*Tel: 268 1242*
Ansett Australia Airlines	*Tel: 13 1300*
Australian Airlines	*Tel: 13 1313*
Eastern Australia Airlines	*Tel: 693 3333*
Eastwest Airlines	*Tel: 268 1166*
Hazelton Airlines	*Tel: 235 1411*

Coaches
Long distance coach travel, for both intra and interstate journeys, can be booked with the following operators:

Bus Australia	*Tel:13 2323*
Greyhound	*Tel:13 1238*
McCafferty's Express	*Tel: 361 5125*
Pioneer Express	*Tel: 13 2030*

Monorail
This privately run service travels in a continuous loop from the city to Darling Harbour and the Chinatown/Haymarket area. The main city stop is at the corner of Pitt and Market Streets.

Taxis
Sydney taxis are plentiful and can either

Ferries offer scenic harbour trips

be hailed on the street or engaged from a cab rank. If you need to book a cab, the major taxi companies are:

Combined Services   *Tel: 332 8888*
Legion Cabs   *Tel: 289 9000*
Premier Radio Cabs   *Tel: 897 4000*
RSL Cabs   *Tel: 699 0144*

Taxis for the disabled can be obtained by calling 339 0200.

Water taxis
If you need private transport anywhere on Sydney Harbour, call Taxis Afloat on 922 4252.

SPORT
See pages 156–161 for full details and addresses.

STUDENT AND YOUTH TRAVEL
International Student Cards are, unfortunately, not a great deal of use in Australia. The cards are not recognised by cinemas, theatres or the State Rail Authority, but you may be able to get concessions on bus travel, and it's worth bringing your card with you, just in case it's useful.

TELEPHONES
Local and STD calls
Public telephones (with clear instructions) for making local and STD calls are found at post offices, phone booths, hotels, shops, stations and cafés. Local calls cost 30 cents (20 and 10 cent pieces) for unlimited time; emergency calls are free. STD calls are cheaper after 6pm every day, and all day Sunday. Dial 012 (0176 from payphones) for operator assistance; 011 for bookings and reverse charge calls.

International calls
It is possible to make international calls from your hotel, some public phones, or from the Telecom Payphone Centre at 100 King Street in the City, which is open 24 hours daily. For enquiries dial 0102; for bookings 0101. Dial 0011 for an international line, followed by the relevant country code:

Canada	1
Ireland	353
New Zealand	64
UK	44
US	1

TICKET AGENCIES
The main booking service for theatre, sporting and music events is **Ticketek**. Credit card bookings can be made on 266 4800, and event enquiries on 266 4848. If you don't have a credit card, Ticketek will direct you to their nearest office, where you can purchase tickets.

Half-price tickets for events can be purchased from the **Halftix** booth in Martin Place (near Elizabeth Street). The catch with this is that tickets are sold only on the day of performance, between 12 noon and 6pm, and there is often a large queue.

TIME
Sydney/NSW is on Australian Eastern Standard Time (AEST), 10 hours ahead of GMT. When it is 12 noon in Sydney it is 2am in London and Dublin, 2pm in Auckland, 5pm in Los Angeles and 8pm in New York.

During the daylight saving period, from October to March, Sydney/NSW is one further hour ahead, ie: 11 hours ahead of GMT.

Note also that AEST is half an hour ahead of Adelaide and Darwin time, and 2 hours ahead of Perth/Western Australian Time.

TIPPING
This is not widely practised in Australia, except in the case of restaurants. Service is not normally added to bills, so a 10 per cent tip, although not obligatory, is acceptable. The tipping of taxi drivers, hotel porters, etc, is at your discretion, and is optional.

TOILETS
Free public toilets are found in parks, public places, galleries and museums, department stores and all bus and train and stations. They are generally clean and well-serviced.

TOURIST OFFICES
NSW Travel Centre, Sydney
Information and bookings for tours, accommodation etc, for Sydney and any area of NSW can be made here. It is located at 19 Castlereagh Street, and is open Monday to Friday from 9am to 5pm. *Tel: 231 4444.* The Centre also provides free maps and information.

Other useful numbers:
Historic Houses Trust *Tel: 692 8366*
National Parks and Wildlife Service *Tel: 585 6333*
National Trust *Tel: 258 0123*
The Rocks Visitor Centre 104 George Street, The Rocks *Tel: 247 4972*
Tourist Information Service *Tel: 669 5111*
Travellers Information Service (Sydney Airport) *Tel: 669 1583/1584*

Regional Tourist Offices
Contact these direct for information on NSW country regions.
Albury *Tel: (060) 21 1477*
Bathurst/Orange *Tel: (063) 33 6288*
Blue Mountains *Tel: (047) 39 6266*
Broken Hill (for all Outback areas)
Tel: (080) 87 6077
Canberra *Tel: (008) 026 166*
Central Coast *Tel: (043) 25 2835*
Coffs Harbour *Tel: (066) 52 1522*
Far South Coast *Tel: (064) 95 3577*
Hunter Valley *Tel: (049) 90 4477*
Lord Howe Island *Tel: 262 6555*
Norfolk Island *Tel: 262 6555*
Port Stephens *Tel: (049) 81 1579*
Richmond/Windsor *Tel: (045) 87 7388*
Snowy Mountains *Tel: (064) 52 1108*
Southern Highlands *Tel: (048) 71 2888*
The Tweed (far north NSW) *Tel: (066) 72 1340*
Wollongong *Tel: (042) 28 0300*

VALETING/LAUNDRY
Most hotels offer a laundry service, although this is usually expensive. Dry-cleaning outlets are widely available throughout the city and country areas. There is also an abundance of laundromats for those who are prepared to do their own washing. Shoeshine services are available at Town Hall Station and in shopping arcades such as the Strand Arcade and the Queen Victoria Building.

Sailing past the Opera House

A
Aboriginal Artists Gallery 54
accommodation 174–5
Adaminaby 124
Admiralty House 27
airport and air
    services 83,176,188
Albury 116
Argyle Place 25, 69
Argyle Street 25, 66,143
Armidale 112–13
Art Gallery of New
    South Wales 54–5,145
Audley 106
Australian Capital
    Territory (ACT) 21,110–11
Australian Museum 62,145
Australian National
    Botanic Gardens 110,137
Australian National
    Maritime Museum 62–3
Australian War Memorial 110
Avalon 37

B
Ballina 118
Balmain 80, 90,146–7
Balmoral Beach 42,138
Balranald 120–1
Batemans Bay 127
Bathurst 112
Bell's Line of Road 39, 96
Ben Boyd National Park 126
Bennelong Point 76
Berrima 40, 108
Bilgola 36
Bilpin 39
Blackheath 39, 96
Blue Mountains
    21, 96–7,134–5,137
Bondi 30–1, 42
Botany Bay 82–3
Bouddi National Park 98
Bourke 120
Bowral 41, 108–9
Braidwood 111
Brisbane Water National Park 98
Broken Hill 121
Bronte Beach 31, 42
Bundanoon 108
Bungendore 111
Byron Bay 118,131

C
Cadman's Cottage 56
Camerons Corner 120
Camp Cove 33
Campbell Parade 30
Campbell's Cove 68
camping 176
Canberra 21, 110–11
Captain Cook's
    Landing Place Historic Site 82
Careening Cove 27
Cattai State Recreation Area 104
Centennial Park 88,136
children in Sydney 154–5,177
Chinatown 48, 145
Church Point 37

Circular Quay 23, 24, 78–9
climate 11, 177
Coastal Scenic Drive 41
Coffs Harbour 118
Collaroy 36
conversion table 178
Coogee Bay 42–3
Cooma 124
Coonabarabran 113
Corowa 116
Cowan Creek 100
Cremorne Point 94,138
crime 179
Cronulla 83, 130
Customs House 78
customs regulations 179

D
Darling Harbour 48–9,145
David Jones'
    Department Store 46, 144
Dawes Point 68
Dee Why 36
disabled travellers 179
the Domain 22–3, 52
Double Bay 90,147
driving 180–1
Drummoyne 93
Durras 127

E
Earth Exchange 63
eating out 86,162–73
Ebenezer 104
Eden 126
Elizabeth Bay 84
Elizabeth Bay House 56, 84
Elizabeth Farm 92
embassies and consulates 181
emergency telephone
    numbers 181
entertainment 148–53, 189
S H Ervin Gallery 55
Experiment Farm Cottage 92–3

F
Farm Cove 53
ferry services 15, 71,188
Fitzroy Falls 41
Five Ways 29
Fort Denison 73

G
The Gap 33
George Street 24–5, 56–7, 64,143
Glebe 90
Glenmore Road 29
Gosford 98, 137
Grafton 118
Griffith 129

H
Harrington Street 25, 65
Hawkesbury River 101,104,132
health matters 182
Heathcote National Park 107
hitch-hiking 182
Hunter Valley 128–9
Hunters Hill 57, 94

Hyde Park 46
Hyde Park Barracks 60, 63

J
James Craig and Kanangra 48
Jamison Valley 39, 97
Jenolan Caves 96
Jervis Bay 126–7,131
Jindabyne 124
Juniper Hall 89

K
Kangaroo Valley 41,109
Katoomba 39, 97
Kiama 41, 109
Kings Cross 84–5
Kingston 115
Kirribilli 27, 95
Kirribilli House 27
Kosciusko National Park 125
Ku-ring-gai Chase
    National Park 100,130–1
Kurnell peninsula 82

L
La Perouse 82–3
Lake Macquarie 99
Lanyon Homestead 111
Leura 39, 97
Lightning Ridge 120
local etiquette 14,181
local time 189
Long Reef 36
Lord Howe Island 21,114
lost property 183
Lower Fort Street 25, 56, 69

M
MacKenzie's Point 31
Macquarie Street 22, 60–1
Manly 34–5, 43
maps 183
Marouba 83
McKell Park 138
McMahon's Point 94–5
media 184
Merimbula 126
Miller's Point 25, 68
Milson's Point 27, 94–5
the Mint 60
Mittagong 40
Moama 116
money 184–5
Monorail 49, 188
Morton National Park 109
Moruya 127
Moss Vale 40–1, 109
Mount Tomah
    Botanic Gardens 137
Mount Victoria 39, 97
Mount Wilson Gardens 137
Mrs Macquarie's
    Point 23, 52–3,138
Mudgee 129
Mungo National Park 121
Murray River 21,116–17,132
Museum of Contemporary
    Art 55, 79
Myall Lakes 119,132

N

Namadgi National Park 111
Narooma 127
Narrabeen 36
Narrabeen lakes 37
National Gallery of Australia 111
national holidays 185
National Trust Centre 66
New England 112–13
New South Wales 10–11, 21
New South Wales State
  Conservatorium of Music 60
Newcastle 98
Newport 36–7
Nielsen Park 33, 43,139
Norfolk Island 21,115
Norman Lindsay Gallery
  and Museum 97
North Head 35

O

Observatory Hill 25, 66
Old Government House 93
opening hours 185
Orange 112
the Outback 21,120–1
Oxford Street 28

P

Paddington
  28–9, 58, 88–9, 90,146,147
Palm Beach 37,101
Parramatta 20, 92–3
Parsley Bay 33
Perisher Valley 125
pharmacies 187
Pitt Town 105
Pittwater 37,100–1, 132
places of worship 187
police 187
Port Hacking 83
Port Jackson 70–1
Port Macquarie 118–19
Port Stephens 119,132
post offices 187
Potts Point 85
Powerhouse Museum 63

public transport 15, 49,188
Pylon Lookout 26, 73
Pyrmont Bridge 49

Q

Quarantine Station 35
Queen Street 29, 89
Queen Victoria Building 46–7,144

R

Richmond 104
Riverina 21, 117
The Rocks 56–7, 64–5,143
Rose Bay 95
Royal Botanic Gardens 23, 53
Royal National Park 106–7,131

S

St Andrews Cathedral 47
St James Church 61
St Mary's Cathedral 47
shopping 142–7
Sir Donald Bradman
  Museum 41,108–9
South Head 33
Snowy Mountains
  21,124–5,134,135
sport 156–61
State Library of New
  South Wales 61
State Parliament House 61
The Story of Sydney 67
student and youth travel 189
Sturt National Park 120
Sutton Forest 41,109
Sydney Cove 79
Sydney Entertainment Centre 49
Sydney Harbour 70–1,133
Sydney Harbour Bridge 26, 72–3
Sydney Harbour
  National Park 33, 35
Sydney Harbour
  National Park Islands 73,139
Sydney Observatory 67
Sydney Opera House 23, 76–7,148
Sydney Tower 47
Sydney Tramway Museum 107

T

Tamarama Bay 31, 43
Tamworth 113
Taylor Square 28
telephones 189
Terrigal 99
Thredbo 125
Three Sisters 39, 97
Tibooburra 120
Tidbinbilla Nature Reserve 111
tipping 190
toilets 190
tourist offices 190
tours, organised 186–7
travelling to Sydney 176–7
Tuggerah Lakes 99
Tweed Heads 118

U

Ulladulla 127
University of Sydney 95

V

Vaucluse House 33,57
Victoria Barracks 89
Vienna Cottage 57
voltage 181

W

Wagga Wagga 113
Walsh Bay 68
Warrumbungle National Park 113
E G Waterhouse National
  Camellia Garden 137
Watsons Bay 33
Wentworth Falls 38, 97
Whale Beach 37
White Cliffs 121
Wilberforce 105
Wilcannia 121
Windsor 105
Wiseman's Ferry 105
Wollongong 41, 109
Woollahra 29, 89
Woolloomooloo 53, 85
words and expressions 182–3

ACKNOWLEDGEMENTS
The Automobile Association would like to thank the following photographers, libraries and associations for their assistance in the preparation of this book.

PAUL KENWARD took all the photographs not mentioned below.
J ALLAN CASH PHOTOLIBRARY p 121 Palace Hotel, Broken Hill
JOHN BORTHWICK p89 Museum of Australian Childhood, p104 St Matthews Anglican Church, p105 Windsor
LONE PINE SANCTUARY p2 and 140 Koala
D McGonigal p114/15 Norfolk Island
MARY EVANS PICTURE LIBRARY p122/3 Hunting Kangaroo, Aborigines
ANNE MATTHEWS p53 Domain Pool and Woolloomooloo Bay, p73 Rocks Building, p96 Kanangra, p164/5 Phillip's Foote Restaurant
NATURE PHOTOGRAPHERS LTD p102/3 Banksia Ericifolius (T Schilling), White Gum, Eucalyptus, coastal Banksia (K J Carlson), Eucalyptus Caesia (T Schilling), p140/1 Laughing Kookaburra, Rainbow Lorikeet
SPECTRUM COLOUR LIBRARY Cover Opera House, p8 Bare Island, p10 Perisher Valley, p102/3 Sign, p106 Royal National Park, NSW, p107 Era Beach, p112/3 Armidale Post Office, p117 Paddle Steamer, p119 Big Banana, Coffs Harbour, p124 Snowy Mountains, p125 Perisher Sunrise, Lake Jindabyne, p126 Fishing Boat, p167 Tai Pan Restaurant, p171 The Corse at Manly